CREATING WELL-BEING:

THE HEALING PATH TO LOVE, PEACE, SELF-ESTEEM AND HAPPINESS

by

Philip H. Friedman, Ph.D.

Published by
R&E PUBLISHERS, INC.
P. O. BOX 2008
SARATOGA, CALIFORNIA 95070
TELEPHONE: 408-866-6303
FAX: 408-866-0825

Library of Congress Card Catalog Number
89-62095

I.S.B.N.
0-88247-841-9

In order to protect the privacy of individuals, couples and families, the names, locations and specific details and circumstances have been changed to some extent in most of the examples given in Creating Well-Being. However, the general accuracy of the content has been maintained in order to give as close to a factual account as possible of experiences of the people described.

The author wishes to thank THE FOUNDATION FOR INNER PEACE in Tiburon, California, for permission to quote from *A COURSE IN MIRACLES*, and S.Y.D.A. FOUNDATION in South Fallsberg, New York, for permission to quote from *WHERE ARE YOU GOING*.

DEDICATION

I dedicate this book to my loving parents, Mickey and Leonard Friedman. Their tremendous love, caring, kindness, resourcefulness, and nurturance from the time of my birth has been given consistently, patiently and generously. They always believed in me, guided me, encouraged me and supported me.

To my sister Elaine and my brothers Jeffrey and David, I also want to share my deepest appreciation for growing up with me and lovingly sharing these many years of my life. To my grandparents, in-laws, aunts, uncles, cousins, nieces and nephews, living and not living, who have loved and nurtured me over the years, I want to express my sincere thanks for their caring and support.

Table of Contents

ACKNOWLEDGEMENTS AND GRATITUDE

I am eternally grateful to the many people and teachers who guided me along the way in the development of the ideas for this

*I AM ETERNALLY GRATEFUL TO THE MANY
PEOPLE AND TEACHERS WHO GUIDED ME
ALONG THE WAY IN THE DEVELOPMENT
OF THE IDEAS FOR THIS BOOK*

book and in its actual writing. Their assistance, guidance, support, compassion, wisdom and love is greatly appreciated. None has been more immediately helpful on a day-to-day basis than my wife, Teresa, who not only edited the entire manuscript but also typed it as well. Without her this book would probably never have been written. I am extremely appreciative, thankful and grateful to her. My son, Mathew, prodded me to expand on the ideas by encouraging me to give clear-cut examples of the principles. Although I initially resisted it, the suggestion was a valuable one and I am grateful for it (and him). My publisher, Bob Reed, has been thoughtful, supportive, caring, fair and generous with his time and I very much appreciate the positive attitude he has had from the time he first contacted me and offered to publish my book.

I am also especially grateful and appreciative to my spiritual teachers or teachings; especially Baba Muktananda, Gurumayi

I AM ALSO ESPECIALLY GRATEFUL
AND APPRECIATIVE TO MY SPIRITUAL
TEACHERS AND TEACHINGS

Chidvilasananda, Paul Tuttle and "Raj", Jach Pursel and "Lazaris", and "A Course in Miracles". Many others, directly or indirectly, have been extremely helpful to me, including Molly Whitehouse, Susan Trout, Gerald Jampolsky, Paul Fenske, Swami Umeshananda, Shanti Gaskins and Swami Satchidananda among others, and I thank them from the bottom of my heart. I also want to thank the following people not already mentioned for the excellent workshops, seminars, courses, or trainings I have taken with them over the last 15 years: Oscar Ichazo (Arica), V. J. Pratap (Sky Yoga), Amrit Desai (Kripalu Yoga), Al Pesso (Psychomotor), Werner Erhard (est), John Roger (Insight), Ken and Gloria Wapnick (A Course in Miracles), Bernard Guerney (Relationship Enhancement), Arnold Patent (Celebration Of Abundance), Alan Cohen (Rising in Love), Stephen Levine (Conscious Living and Conscious Dying), Evelyn Isadore and Karen Hughes (Inner Guidance), Shosana Shay (Reiki-Radiance), Ellen Sokolow Molinari (Reiki-II), Robert Fritz (DMA), Herb Kaufmann, Sylvia Lafair and Pat Rodegast (A Day with Emmanuel), J. Z. Knight (A Day with Ramtha), Mietek and Margaret Wirkus (Bioenergy) and Sharon Butler (Hellerwork). I have learned something valuable from every one of them and am grateful to all of them for being in my life.

I HAVE LEARNED SOMETHING VALUABLE FROM
EVERY ONE OF THEM AND AM GRATEFUL
TO ALL OF THEM FOR BEING IN MY LIFE

I am appreciative of all the wisdom and guidance I received from my psychology and psychiatry professors along the way, including Arnold Lazarus, Ivan Boszormenyi-Nagy, Jim Framo,

Gerald Zuk, Leon Robinson, Carl Whitaker, Barclay Martin, Brendan Maher, Len Berkowitz, Vernon Allen, and Fred Keller.

I am also grateful to the editors of the magazines that have published parts of earlier versions of this book: Ruth Hoskins (Wholistic Health Connections), Swami Virato (New Frontier), Jack and Cai Underhill (Life-Times), Paul and Pat Fenske (Spiritual Frontiers), Alan Tillotson (Journal of Well-Being), Brian Williams (Unicorn), and Edie and Michael Weinstein-Moser (Visions). I am also very appreciative of the media who have interviewed me for numerous radio, television and newspaper shows or articles. These include Darrell Sifford and Bill Thompson of the Philadelphia Inquirer newspaper, Murray Needleman (Lifestyles, WWDB radio), David Reed (Getting Together, WCAU radio), Djuna Wojton (Paradigms, WXPN radio), Dan Gottleib (Family Matters, WHYY radio), Jill Chernekoff (Newsprobe, WTAF-TV) and Dorie Lenz (Delaware Valley Forum, WPHL-TV). The media have been very supportive of my work and ideas and I am very thankful to them for their interest and enthusiasm.

THE MEDIA HAVE BEEN VERY SUPPORTIVE
OF MY WORK AND IDEAS AND
I AM VERY THANKFUL TO THEM
FOR THEIR INTEREST AND ENTHUSIASM

I am especially grateful and appreciative for the love and support I have received from the Siddha Meditation and Yoga Centers in Philadelphia and South Fallsburg, New York, and from the continuing, ongoing love, caring, nurturance, fun and support I have received and continue to receive from my friends over the years: Bill and Francie Pagell, Bruce and Cathy Fay,

I AM ESPECIALLY GRATEFUL AND APPRECIATIVE
FOR THE ONGOING LOVE, NURTURANCE,
FUN, AND SUPPORT I HAVE RECEIVED
FROM MY FRIENDS

Jacqueline McDonald, Bob and Nancy Dreyfus, Candace McCoy and John Mahoney, Rita Borzillo, Bob Rosenthal and Pat Fields, Joan Sikora, Kimberly Paterson, Gary and Rebecca Barton, John and Loretta Alex, Michael Carver, Mary Lou Jacoby, Rudi and Sharon Bauer, Rod and Diane Boggs, Pat Fort, Michael and Johanna Wald, Jack McMullen, Paula Amar, Mary Lee Goldberg, Frank Guarnaccia, David Berg, David Moultrup, Lois Ewert, Kathy Scherbner, Bob Sullivan, Beverly Reinmuller, Ann Hinkel, Jeane Bengtson, Nancy Schmidt, Nora Coffey, Ruth Pagell, Nettie Neumeister, Marianne Strehle, Richard Stanton, Veronica Bukowski, Mercedes Turner, Randy Rolfe, Ray and Peggy Sterner, Ross and Marianne Buck, Father Ryezek, and Talia de Lone, and from my brother and sister-in-law, Eric Stone and Marguerite Friedman. They have shared the personal, professional or spiritual growth path with me.

To all my co-members of the Psychology/Spirituality Interest Group (not previously mentioned) who have met monthly for seven years (Ken Barber, Ruth and Jim Richards, Steve Dougherty, Jack Porter, Sandy Shemonski, Barbara Good, Gary Lord, Anne Kinnier, David Knotts, Richard Neville and James Saxon, among others), I am also very thankful and appreciative. I also want to thank all my clients and seminar participants who have shared their struggles, pains, fears, hopes, desires, goals and successes with me and who have been both my teachers and students. I am especially grateful to my mother and father-in-law, Ollie and Chloe Molinaro, and to Shirley Molinaro for their love, support and encouragement, and to my brother-in-law, George Molinaro, whose sudden death had such a profound effect on all our lives.

I want to thank all the people I have previously mentioned for not only their contribution to my life but also for the wonderful work they are doing and have been doing in the world to make it a better place.

I WANT TO THANK ALL THE PEOPLE
I HAVE PREVIOUSLY MENTIONED FOR

*NOT ONLY THEIR CONTRIBUTION TO MY LIFE
BUT ALSO FOR THE WONDERFUL WORK
THEY ARE DOING AND HAVE BEEN DOING
IN THE WORLD TO MAKE IT A BETTER PLACE*

In addition, I am grateful, in advance, to all the distributors, sales agents, bookstores and my publisher for promoting and selling this book, and to all of you who are investing your time and money to buy and read it. It is my fervent desire that the value you receive from reading this book contributes substantially to your wisdom and upliftment, and to your personal and spiritual well-being.

*IT IS MY FERVENT DESIRE THAT THE VALUE
YOU RECEIVE FROM READING THIS BOOK
CONTRIBUTES SUBSTANTIALLY TO YOUR
UPLIFTMENT AND WISDOM AND TO YOUR
PERSONAL AND SPIRITUAL WELL-BEING*

"Teach only love, for that is what you are." –*A Course in Miracles, p. 87*

"Only when a person turns within and becomes immersed in his own inner Self can he truly experience love." –*Where Are You Going?, p. 43*

"The only way to have peace is to teach peace. By teaching peace you must learn it yourself. . ." –*A Course in Miracles, p. 92*

"What do we want? We want happiness. . . But if we were to truly examine ourselves, then we would discover that the happiness we are looking for can be found only within us." –*Where Are You Going?, p. 9*

PREFACE

It is no accident that you are reading this book and it is no accident that I wrote it. You were guided to read this book just as I was guided to write it. You have perceived and experienced

IT IS NO ACCIDENT THAT YOU ARE READING THIS BOOK AND IT IS NO ACCIDENT THAT I WROTE IT. YOU WERE GUIDED TO READ THIS BOOK JUST AS I WAS GUIDED TO WRITE IT.

many people and events as distressing in your life and that drove you to search for a better way to live. The experiences and people that I perceived as distressing and upsetting in my life also drove me to search for a better way to live. These experiences triggered my start on a psychology/personal growth path and later, onto a spiritual path. Even though, at the time, certain experiences were upsetting to me and generated feelings of hurt, anger, fear, grief, and guilt, in retrospect, I am grateful for them. They included career and relationship conflicts during my first three jobs at three different professional institutions; neck, back and shoulder pains; the sudden death of my brother-in-law George (35) in a hotel fire in 1980; and the subsequent grief and life-threatening illness my wife Teresa survived in 1982. During each life crisis, I learned more profound lessons about myself, relationships, the spiritual journey, and what is necessary for an enduring level of high well-being. At the same time I was moving through several stages of my life; such as, "settling down", "becoming my own person", and

DURING EACH LIFE CRISES I LEARNED
MORE PROFOUND LESSONS

the "mid-life transition". I learned that peace, joy, happiness, love, creativity and well-being ultimately can only be found within one's own Self/Being.

At 47, I have been practicing psychology for over 20 years, since receiving my Ph.D. in clinical psychology from the University of Wisconsin, where Teresa and I met and immediately fell in love. My interest and involvement with spirituality started four years later in 1972 and for the last ten years, I have attempted to integrate psychology and spirituality not only into my personal life but also into my writing, teaching and therapy. For many years I have trained and taught other professionals in the helping professions: psychologists, psychiatry residents, social workers, school counselors, marriage and family therapists, nurses, teachers, and students in training of various kinds. I have also conducted workshops and courses for the general public as well as for industry, colleges and schools.

I am a psychologist in full-time private practice and an Assistant Professor at Hahnemann Medical School and University. I am also the Executive Director of the Foundation for Well-Being and the Director of the Attitudinal Healing Center of the Delaware Valley in Pennsylvania (Philadelphia and surrounding area). In all these endeavors, I have tried to integrate a psychological and spiritual approach to life and well-being. This book, then, is an integrative, psycho-spiritual approach to creating and enhancing well-being. It is based on the "12 Core Principles of Well-Being": the 12 steps, building blocks, or foundations of well-being.

THIS BOOK IS AN INTEGRATIVE, PSYCHO-SPIRITUAL APPROACH TO CREATING AND ENHANCING WELL-BEING

In both my private practice of psychotherapy and in my seminars, I meditate before conducting the sessions. I quiet my mind, ask for guidance from the creative/infinite intelligence (the divine/holy spirit or energy), bless each person I see and ask that I(we) be an instrument of divine love. I, or my assistants and I, ask that we be guided to be helpful in ways that will be most healing and for the highest good of everyone involved. I ask that all barriers, blocks and obstacles to healing be removed for all of us

WE ASK THAT WE BE GUIDED TO BE HELPFUL IN WAYS THAT WILL BE MOST HEALING AND FOR THE HIGHEST GOOD OF EVERYONE INVOLVED

and that we be allowed to join together under the guidance of a higher power to learn how to release fear, anger, hurt, guilt, judgments and negative attitudes, to learn how to forgive ourselves and others, and to learn how to love ourselves and others unconditionally. My assistants and I frequently join hands before a seminar begins and, with our eyes closed, ask for guidance. We visualize the members of the group, including ourselves, surrounded and joined by a radiant, loving and healing light. I will

WE VISUALIZE EVERYONE SURROUNDED BY A RADIANT, LOVING LIGHT

sometimes do this in therapy sessions with those clients who are open, receptive and interested in this kind of healing invocation or guidance. Generally, when we join together in this way, all people involved experience it as uplifting, inspiring, and healing. I would like to invite you now to close your eyes, surround yourself with a radiant white light, and ask the creative/infinite intelligence (divine/holy spirit or energy) to help you get maximum value out of reading this book.

ASK THE CREATIVE/INFINITE INTELLIGENCE (DIVINE/HOLY SPIRIT) TO HELP YOU GET MAXIMUM VALUE OUT OF READING THIS BOOK

(Before reading the book, you may find it helpful to fill out the three questionnaires listed in Appendix I, II, and III; i.e., the Well-Being Questionnaire, the Well-Being Scale, and the Stress Reaction Questionnaire.

There are many profound ideas presented in this book. As you read and study them, you will find that your interest in a particular idea will magnetize you to similar ideas presented by other

THERE ARE MANY PROFOUND IDEAS PRESENTED IN THIS BOOK

authors in slightly different ways until you have mastered the idea and successfully applied it to your life. The central teaching of this book, however, is that the core of a human being is the Self or Being whose essence is love. Therefore, on the journey to "well-being", we need to find the Self/Being within which exists as

THE CENTRAL TEACHING OF THIS BOOK IS THAT THE CORE OF A HUMAN BEING IS THE SELF OR BEING WHOSE ESSENCE IS LOVE

us. We also need to learn how to see the Self/Being in each other. In other words, we need to find and accept the love within ourselves and we need to seek and discover the love in others. In so doing, we will dramatically enhance our well-being and the well-being of others. This book is designed to help you on the journey to enhance your well-being; and perhaps some day you will be a guide, teacher, or catalyst for the well-being of someone else. Good luck on that journey. May the force of the creative/infinite intelligence (divine/holy spirit or energy) be with you.

CHAPTER ONE

CREATING AND DEVELOPING A SENSE OF PURPOSE AND VISION IN LIFE

You can transform the quality of your well-being, your mental health and your life. You can be the pilot of the plane, the captain of the ship. By clarifying your purpose and vision in life in alignment with your true Self, the core of your Being, you can and will initiate a powerful and exiting process leading to an enriching and uplifting lifelong goal. There are 12 guidelines for creating and developing a sense of purpose and vision in life.

1. **WELL-BEING/MENTAL HEALTH** Creating and developing a sense of purpose and vision in life is the first essential

IMAGINE THAT YOU ARE THE CAPTAIN OF THE SHIP
AND YOU HAVE TO CHART THE COURSE
OF YOUR ENTIRE LIFE

ingredient for a high state of well-being and mental health. It is as if you were the captain of a ship and had to create a destination that would chart the course of your entire life. You would need to have a vision of who you were and where you wanted to go before planning the journey. A clearly defined sense of purpose, like a very long-range goal, serves that function. Moreover, people with the highest states of well-being and mental health generally have purposes that focus both on the present and the future. They experience themselves deeply. They see beyond themselves. Reflect for a short time on your long-range purpose and vision in life.

2. **MEANING/DIRECTION** A sense of purpose and a vision of who you are and where you want to go give meaning and direction to your life. Instead of bobbing along on the currents of your life, you will discover that your life is meaningful, valuable, purposeful, and has a constructive direction to it. You will also begin to see how your life fits into a larger picture of all people on the planet. Reflect on the meaning and direction of your life for a few minutes.

3. **FORCE/ENERGY** A purpose and a vision in life not only give you a sense of meaning and direction, they also serve as a unifying force, organizing, balancing and harmonizing all your energies. In this way, they integrate all aspects of your self, energies and life, and bring your diverse needs, desires and goals together under one central focus. Reflect for a few minutes on the unifying, organizing, integrating, balancing and harmonizing energy or force in your life. Write a summary of your reflections on steps 1, 2, and 3.

4. **VALUES/BELIEFS** The long-range sense of purpose and vision in life is directly related to core values and beliefs about yourself, relationships, career, vocation, education, personal and spiritual growth, life, the universe and God. For example, if you believe that your essence is love (or good) and you live in a loving universe, your sense of purpose and vision is likely to be very different than if you believe your essence is evil or bad and you live in a fearful universe. Reflect for a short time on your core values and believes.

5. **ASPIRATIONS/DREAMS** Your long-range aspirations and dreams will be guided on one hand by your core beliefs and values and on the other hand by your purpose and vision in life. What you aspire to, what you dream of, connects with your deepest longings and desires. Your wants and goals are

WHAT YOU ASPIRE TO, WHAT YOU DREAM OF,
CONNECTS WITH YOUR DEEPEST
LONGINGS AND DESIRES

largely determined by these aspirations and dreams. Generally, people with high levels of well-being and mental health set high aspirations and long-range dreams for themselves and their life. Reflect on your highest aspirations and dreams in life.

6. **MOTIVATION/INTENTION** Your purpose and vision in life, when aligned with your aspirations, dreams and core values and beliefs, motivate you to action. Motivation means to set in motion, to energize. The direction of movement is set by your intentions. Your intentions, in turn, indicate your

MOTIVATION MEANS TO SET IN MOTION,
TO ENERGIZE. THE DIRECTION OF MOVEMENT
IS SET BY YOUR INTENTIONS

direction, usually why you are moving in that direction and what you hope to accomplish when you arrive at your destination. Reflect on your motivations and intentions in life and how they are aligned with your aspirations, dreams, core values and beliefs. In a short paragraph, write your current understanding and awareness of your core values and beliefs.

7. **QUALITIES/CHARACTERISTICS** You have a unique set of positive qualities or characteristics. The combination of qualities or characteristics you have are unique to you and can help you to express your purpose and vision in life.

Reflect on your unique combination of qualities and characteristics. List three or four of your most positive ones on a piece of paper.

8. **ABILITIES/SKILLS** You have a unique set of positive abilities, skills, talents and resources within you which represent an inherent diamond mine of treasures given to you by the Creator or Creative Process. When identified, they represent what you love to do when naturally expressing yourself in alignment with your purpose and vision in life. Reflect on your unique abilities, skills, talents or resources. List three or four of them that you especially like.

9. **SERVICE/CONTRIBUTION** Your highest purpose and vision in life may be served by expressing your uniqueness in a way that also serves other people's lives. This "awareness of contribution" to others begins to elevate your sense of purpose and vision beyond yourself. People with high levels of

YOUR HIGHEST PURPOSE AND VISION
MAY BE SERVED BY EXPRESSING YOUR
UNIQUENESS IN A WAY THAT ALSO
SERVES OTHER PEOPLE'S LIVES

well-being and mental health are usually aware of the ways their skills, abilities, talents, resources, qualities and characteristics are being used to serve and contribute to other's lives. Reflect on how your expression of what you love to do can begin to contribute to others. Write down your current awareness and understanding.

10. **SYMBOLS/IMAGES** Often your deepest and highest sense of purpose and vision in life can be accessed through symbols and images. Spend five minutes practicing a relaxation or meditation exercise with your eyes closed. Take slow, deep breaths. Listen to your inner voice. What is it telling you? How is it guiding you? Then ask for an image or symbol to

enter your consciousness to represent your deepest or highest sense of purpose and vision. Surround that image or symbol with a radiant white light and bring it gently into your heart. Feel, sense and smell the symbol and image. Have an inner dialogue with it. Talk to it. Let it talk to you. If you have difficulty the first time, be compassionate with yourself and try again later. Reflect on the meaning and significance of your image and symbol. Request, before going to sleep at night, that you have a dream that will reveal your deepest and highest purpose and vision. Write down what you experienced during the relaxation, meditation and dream process.

11. **MISSION/CALLING** Your deepest and highest purpose and vision in life will fulfill your deepest core values and beliefs and be most in alignment with the essence of your Being. By fully expressing yourself in alignment with your Being, you will not only be fulfilling the deepest core of your Being, you will also be responding to a deeper calling or mission within you. You will be expressing your unique qualities in a way that maximally contributes to and benefits others. Reflect on all the previous steps and how you can fulfill and align your purpose and vision in life with a sense of mission or calling. Write down your understanding and awareness.

12. **SELF/BEING** Many spiritual traditions agree that at the essence or core of your Being is the Higher or Inner Self. Some refer to this as the Inner Light, the Inner Christ, Buddha, Shiva or Jehovah, the Kingdom of Heaven within, etc. This essence consists of the experience of profound Joy, Love, Peace, Creativity, Light, Truth, Freedom and Beauty. On your journey through life, the highest purpose or vision may be to align yourself with the essence of your Being, the Self or Consciousness. By doing this, you fulfill your true Self and

*THE HIGHEST PURPOSE OR VISION MAY BE
TO ALIGN YOURSELF WITH THE ESSENCE
OF YOUR BEING, THE SELF
OR CONSCIOUSNESS*

express your highest purpose and vision in life. In the process, you also experience the highest level of well-being for yourself; i.e., deep love, peace, and joy, and maximally serve and contribute to others. Reflect on your deepest, truest sense of Being, Self and Consciousness and on how your highest purpose and vision in life would be fulfilling your deepest core values and beliefs. Reflect on how expressing your unique qualities, characteristics, abilities, skills, talents, and resources would fulfill your highest purpose and vision in life. Now write a three to four sentence, concise, focused statement on your purpose and vision.

Frequently read your statement of purpose and vision, preferably once a day. Review and, if necessary, revise your statement of purpose and vision at least once per year.

EXAMPLES OF PURPOSE AND VISION IN LIFE

"My deepest and highest vision in life is to create peace and love universally and to achieve a simplicity in life whereby peace and love could be shared by all and not only a few."

(Financial Analyst)

"My purpose and vision in life is to develop several centers nationwide devoted to healing one's whole being, physically, emotionally and spiritually."

(Food Store Assistant Manager)

"My purpose and vision in life is to use my intelligence and patience to perceive my true Self and to assist others in this pursuit by listening, advocating and educating others regarding their highest Self."

(Juvenile Justice Lawyer)

"My purpose and vision in life is to learn self-acceptance and to help others accept themselves by using my vulnerability, honesty, self-appraisal, courage and acceptance to teach, counsel, facilitate, serve, help and write."

(Prison Counselor)

"My purpose and vision in life is to be happy, creative and loving and to use my qualities of honesty, determination, fairness, resourcefulness and originality and my manual dexterity, mechanical aptitude, mathematical, organizing and design skills to create worthwhile products and to serve others."

(Engineering Lab Technician)

"My purpose and vision in life is to use my intelligence, understanding, perseverance and communication ability to design and construct beautiful and useful buildings and homes that benefit others and, in the process, create a happy, organized, balanced and successful life for me and my family."

(Builder)

"My purpose and vision in life is to use my love, intelligence, compassion, and professional expertise to serve others and assist them in healing physically, emotionally and spiritually."

(Physician)

"My purpose and vision in life is to actualize myself; to play up to my par in my judgment, not society's or anyone else's; to know that I've connected with a good number of people in ways that helped them and me through my newspaper columns, the books I write and my public speaking engagements; and to achieve a high degree of tranquility."

(Newspaper Columnist and Author)

PURPOSE/VISION
HOME WORK/PLAY SHEET

1. LIST SOME OF YOUR UNIQUE, PERSONAL QUALITIES (such as: Intelligence, Curiosity, Determination, Creativity, Love, Enthusiasm, Humor, etc.)

    A.

    B.

    C.

    D.

    E.

2. LIST SOME OF YOUR SKILLS, TALENTS AND ABILITIES (such as: Serving/Helping others, Instructing, Educating, Leading, Organizing, Directing, Planning, Creating, Designing and Arranging, Writing, Fixing, etc.)

    A.

    B.

    C.

    D.

    E.

3. WRITE DOWN YOUR LONG-RANGE GOAL IN LIFE (i.e., Over 20 to 40 years, such as happiness, love, joy, fulfillment, excitement, pleasure, satisfaction, mastery, creative expression, fun, etc.)

    _____

    _____

    _____

    _____

4. IMAGINE THAT THERE WERE NO OBSTACLES OR HURDLES IN YOUR LIFE. YOU CAN WAVE A MAGIC WAND AND CREATE A PERFECT LIFE. WHAT WOULD IT "LOOK AND FEEL" LIKE IF YOU FULFILLED YOUR PURPOSE AND VISION?

    _____

    _____

    _____

    _____

5.   CLOSE YOUR EYES. RELAX. TAKE A FEW DEEP BREATHS. ALLOW AN IMAGE OR SYMBOL TO ENTER YOUR CONSCIOUSNESS THAT REPRESENTS YOUR DEEPEST OR HIGHEST SENSE OF PURPOSE AND VISION. HAVE AN INNER DIALOGUE WITH THE SYMBOL OR IMAGE.   THEN WRITE DOWN YOUR IMAGE, SYMBOL AND DIALOGUE.

_____

_____

_____

6.   COMBINE THE PREVIOUS FIVE STEPS INTO A ONE PARAGRAPH STATEMENT. (Example: My purpose and vision in life is to use my intelligence, creativity, determination, curiosity and love to create the highest possible levels of well-being for myself, my family, friends, clients and students, plus organizations and society. I plan to do this by using the following skills, talents and abilities that I possess:

1)   Serving, helping, empathizing;
2)   Instructing and educating;
3)   Innovating, leading, directing;
4)   Organizing and executing;
5)   Researching and investigating;

OR
6)   Creating and developing;
7)   Persuading and influencing;
8)   Writing and publishing;
9)   Uplifting and inspiring;
10)   Envisioning and manifesting.)

_____

_____

_____

_____

_____

_____

_____

CHAPTER TWO

THE CREATION AND MANIFESTATION PROCESS: GUIDELINES FOR CREATING AND MANIFESTING WHAT YOU WANT (YOUR GOALS) IN LIFE

The following twelve guidelines are powerful steps to help you attain what you want – your goals in life. I recommend that you precede using these twelve guidelines by first engaging in a short, effective meditative/relaxation procedure such as the "Meditation/Relaxation Journey to the Inner Sanctuary" (see process that follows the example). Both seminar participants and private clients with whom I work find this simple meditative/relaxation procedure very peaceful and healing in its own right.

1. **PURPOSE/VISION** Develop a sense of clarity about your purpose and vision in life. Reflect for a moment on your highest, long-term aspirations and dreams; not only for yourself but also for other people. Think about your unique skills, talents, abilities and resources and how you can use them to serve yourself and other people as well. Reflect on the long-range sense of meaning and direction in your life, and then

state to your self or, preferably, write down your purpose and vision, briefly and succinctly, in one to three sentences.

2. **WANTS/GOALS** Become very clear about what you want for yourself in the near future (e.g., 3 to 4 months) and convert this want into a specific goal. The goal may be related to your

CLARIFY YOUR WANTS, YOUR GOALS
FOR YOURSELF

career, your physical, emotional, psychological, financial or spiritual health or well-being, your relationships (family, friends, work), leisure activities, and so forth. Be specific, clear and brief. If the specific want or goal is aligned with your larger purpose and vision in life, it will be much more powerful. Write the goal on a piece of paper. Read it often.

3. **DESIRE/FEELING** Allow yourself to feel how intensely you want this goal. Create or find within you the burning desire you have for the goal. In order to create what you want,

CREATE OR FIND THE BURNING DESIRE
YOU HAVE FOR THE GOAL

you will need to energize the creation process. When you feel or desire something strongly, you will create the energy and momentum necessary to achieve it. Dominant thoughts and goals require intense desires and feelings to energize and activate them, and to create the drive for attaining the sought after goal.

4. **VISUALIZE/IMAGINE** Visualize attaining your goal within a reasonable period of time in the near future (e.g., 3-4 months). Imagine yourself reaching the goal, the want, as if it were taking place right now. Feel the goal, sense it, touch

IMAGINE YOURSELF REACHING THE GOAL
RIGHT NOW

it, smell it, even taste it, as if you had already attained the goal in the present. Then alternate back and forth three or four times or more in your visualization and imagination between your current reality situation and the experience of attaining your goal. Finally, visualize your current reality situation and the attainment of your goal simultaneously as if they were on a split video screen. This creates a healthy discrepancy or dissonance that will further motivate you to attain your goal.

5. **CHOICE/DECISION** Make a conscious choice, a conscious

MAKE A CONSCIOUS CHOICE
TO ATTAIN YOUR GOAL

decision to attain your goal. While you are visualizing the attainment of your goal in the near future, say several times to yourself, "I choose to create this goal (fill in the goal) for myself". Then repeat these affirmations twice each to yourself: "The past is over." "Now is the only time there is." "Now is the key to the future." "Now is the most important moment of my life." "Now I am the predominant creative force in my life." "Now I choose to create this goal for myself." Visualize the goal attained. Then state twice to yourself: "Now I choose to be true to myself."

6. **BENEFITS/RESULTS** Visualize a point in time one year from now (the future-future). You have attained and experienced your goal for about nine months. Allow yourself to reflect on all the positive benefits you will have experienced over this nine month period as a result of having attained your goal. Reflect on all the positive results you have created for yourself. Reflect on any enhanced or fringe benefits that will come to you or anyone else in your life as a result of creating your goal in the near future. Feel the enthusiasm, excitement and satisfaction that comes with this awareness.

7. **ACKNOWLEDGEMENT/GRATITUDE** Imagine that it is one year from now (future-future). Acknowledge yourself for having created what you wanted, your goal, at the near future point in time (3-4 months) and for creating all these benefits in your life. Allow yourself to feel a deep sense of gratitude to yourself for creating your goal and the benefits of attaining it. Allow yourself to feel a deep sense of gratitude toward all those people who supported you in attaining your goal; both the people currently in your life and the ones who will enter your life in the coming months in order to support you. More miracles occur from gratitude (and forgiveness) than from anything else.

MORE MIRACLES OCCUR FROM GRATITUDE (AND FORGIVENESS) THAN FROM ANYTHING ELSE

8. **COMMITMENT/PERSISTENCE** Commit yourself 100 percent to the attainment of your goal, for the moment one commits oneself, the universe moves, too. All sorts of unforeseen events, people, situations, meetings, and opportunities begin to happen to help you attain your goal once you

THE MOMENT ONE COMMITS ONESELF THE UNIVERSE MOVES TOO

are totally committed to it. Persist until the goal has been accomplished. Many of the greatest successes and achievements have been reached following temporary setbacks, defeats and disappointments. Perseverance along with commitment ensures the success and completion of the goal.

9. **FAITH/TRUST** Reflect on that part of yourself which has total faith and trust that the goal will be attained. You already have an intense desire to attain your goal and have chosen to create it. Now you are permitting yourself to completely trust that you will achieve it. This vital faith can be in

yourself, the universe or in creative/infinite intelligence. The power of faith and trust in yourself, in the universe and in creative/infinite intelligence will greatly accelerate your attaining your goal.

THE POWER OF FAITH AND TRUST WILL GREATLY
ACCELERATE ATTAINING YOUR GOAL

10. **ACTIONS/PLAN** Decide on the initial action steps you are going to take to attain your goal. These first few steps will begin to create momentum toward the completion of your goal. It is helpful to first visualize yourself taking these preliminary action steps. This generates positive energy toward the attainment of the goal. Create an image in your mind of the initial plan you are going to develop to reach your goal. You may want to modify or adjust the plan later as you go along. In fact, you will probably create a plan, take initial action steps, receive inner and outer feedback, then adjust and create again; create, then act, receive feedback and adapt; create, act, receive feedback and adjust; create, act, receive feedback and adapt, always keeping your eye on the goal. Remember to keep in focus how your actions can be of service to others.

11. **HIGHEST GOOD/INFINITE INTELLIGENCE** Ask that a higher power or force, such as infinite, universal or creative intelligence, help you to attain your goal. Ask that the attainment of your goal be for your highest good and for the highest

ASK THAT THE GOAL BE FOR
YOUR HIGHEST GOOD

good of all the people involved. Furthermore, ask the creative/infinite intelligence to help you either attain this goal, or if this goal is not for your highest good, to help you attain another goal that is more aligned with your highest good and highest purpose in life.

12. **SURRENDER/LOVE** Surrender your goal to this higher power or force. This means you need to mentally and emotionally let it go, release it and turn it over to this force or power. This higher power or force is often referred to as the higher or inner Self, the inner Voice, inner Light, inner Master or Teacher, Inner Being, Holy Spirit, Kundalini en-

*SURRENDER THE GOAL TO THIS HIGHER POWER
OR FORCE*

ergy, or God. The important thing is that you let go of and surrender the goal to this higher power or force. While you are doing this, connect with that part of you that experiences love. Deep within you, at the core of your Self/Being, is the experience of love. Allow this love for yourself, for other people, for the universe, or for God, to flow through you and

AT THE CORE OF YOUR SELF/BEING IS LOVE

to align itself with the wisdom of creative/infinite intelligence.

Repeat steps 1 through 12 frequently, preferably once a day. Step by step, gradually, and sometimes dramatically, you will create and manifest your goals in life.

Jim, a 30 year old graduate student, was single and living alone. He had not dated in six years, had no friends, and little self-confidence or self-esteem. He lifted weights occasionally and was physically fit. Nonetheless, he was shy and withdrawn. His father had either been murdered or committed suicide while his mother was pregnant with him. His only semi-close relationships was with one sister. He disliked his stepfather and had a cool but cordial relationship with his mother. I decided to teach him the meditation/relaxation and creation and manifestation exercises which he practiced diligently. He read, reread and studied the 12 steps of this process and kept visualizing what he wanted. His immediate goal was to meet a woman his age and develop a relationship.

A month later, Jim went to a social event late one Saturday night. While having a beer, he noticed a young woman at the other end of the hall looking at him. He struck up a conversation with her. They chatted briefly but she clearly wasn't interested in him. He moved away. Rather than feel hurt and rejected, he noticed another woman, Collette, playing a video game in the adjoining room. He went over and challenged her to a game. She accepted. They played a few games and then talked for nearly two hours. Jim invited her back to his apartment for "breakfast", which she accepted. They spent an intimate night together. Although he tried to contact Collette again, it didn't work out. But he kept visualizing what he wanted. Two weeks later, he approached another woman at a different social function and was turned down. Soon after this, he saw a young woman at the jukebox. He looked toward her. She said something and they started talking. Several hours later, she agreed to spend the night with him at his apartment and dated him several times. In the meantime he met and dated Nancy, who was in one of his classes at school.

Although Jim experienced two rejections, he dated three women and had six dates over a 10 week period of time. His self-esteem and self-confidence started to improve markedly. During the next 8 weeks, Jim went out with several women while he continued to practice visualizing himself meeting and interacting with women using the "creating and manifesting" process as a guideline. One female graduate student at school even invited him out for a date. He was thrilled. Finding that he preferred her as a friend, however, he chose to gently tell her that she was more interested in him than he was in her.

During four and one half months of therapy, he proved a willing student. He worked on letting go of negative images and self-talk which he had learned during his high school days when he had come to believe he was stupid and inadequate. By learning to release these rejecting images and labels, Jim was able to think of himself as adequate, competent and of above-average intelligence. At the end of therapy, Jim had greatly increased his self-esteem and was planning to enhance his education and training by taking advanced courses in his field of work.

CREATION AND MANIFESTATION PROCESS: SHORT FORM

After you're familiar with using the twelve step process of the "Creation and Manifestation" exercise, you may use a shorter version on a daily basis, assuming that you have already reflected on your purpose and vision in life and have made a summary statement of it.

SIX STEP PROCESS OF CREATION AND MANIFESTATION: SHORT FORM

1. WANTS/GOALS: Get clear about what you want in the near future (1, 3, 6 months). Create a specific goal or series of goals for yourself. Write each goal down. Read it daily.

2. BELIEFS/DESIRES: Allow yourself to strongly believe and expect that you can and will attain your goal. Strongly and intensely desire the attainment of your goal. Feel it; sense it.

3. VISUALIZE/IMAGINE: Visualize or picture yourself attaining your goal as if it were taking place in the present, this instant. Imagine yourself experiencing the goal right now in the present moment. Go back and forth in your mind between current reality and the attainment of the goal, at least 3-4 times.

4. CHOICE/DECISION: Consciously choose to attain your goal. Make a firm, clear decision that you will persist until you've attained your goal, in spite of obstacles, delays, or apparent difficulties.

5. BENEFITS/GRATITUDE: Picture yourself experiencing the benefits of attaining your goal not only in the near future

but also in the future-future. Be grateful to yourself and all the other people who will help you attain your goal.

6. TRUST/INFINITE INTELLIGENCE: Trust that your goal will be attained. Ask creative/infinite intelligence to either help you attain your goal or, if the goal is not for your highest good, to help you attain another goal more aligned with your highest purpose and vision in life.

Use this six step process whenever you are discouraged or upset about the direction of your life or your movement toward your goals. Also use it on a daily basis when you awake in the morning and before going to sleep at night.

SUMMARY OF THE SIX STEP PROCESS

1. **WANTS/GOALS**

2. **BELIEFS/DESIRES**

3. **VISUALIZE/IMAGINE**

4. **CHOICE/DECISION**

5. **BENEFITS/GRATITUDE**

6. **TRUST/INFINITE INTELLIGENCE**

MEDITATION/RELAXATION JOURNEY TO THE INNER SANCTUARY

Close your eyes. Relax. Get in a comfortable, open body position with your arms and legs uncrossed so the energy can flow more easily and smoothly. Pay attention to your breath. Be aware of your breath as you breathe in and out slowly and deeply, slowly and deeply. Breathing in and out slowly and deeply, slowly and deeply. Focus on your breath. Breathing slowly and deeply. Now allow yourself to repeat the word "calm" on the in-breath, and "relax" on the out-breath. Continue to repeat the word "calm" on the in-breath, and "relax" on the out-breath. "Calm" on the in-breath and "relax" on the out-breath. Breathing in "calm" and breathing out "relaxed". Breathing in "calm" and out "relaxed".

Now continue to breathe slowly and deeply on the in-breath and out-breath but this time hold your breath for a count of three between the in-breath and the out-breath. So you are breathing in "calm", holding your breath for a count of three, and breathing out "relaxed".

In just a few moments, you're going to take an elevator ride down from the tenth floor to the first floor. As you go down the elevator from the tenth floor to the first floor, you're going to become even more and more calm and relaxed. . . .deeper and deeper. . . .calmer and calmer. . . .more and more deeply relaxed. Now picture yourself on the tenth floor of an elevator. Slowly the elevator descends from the tenth floor to the first floor. From 10 to 9, 9 to 8, 8 to 7, the elevator slowly descends and as it does, you become so calm, so deeply relaxed, deeper and deeper. . . .calmer and calmer. . . .The elevator continues to descend further, from 7 to 6, 6 to 5, and 5 to 4 and, as it does, you continue to descend further and further inside of yourself to the core, the center of your Being, the place of deep calm, peace, joy, strength, light, love and well-being.

Relaxing even further. . .calmer and calmer. . .more and more deeply relaxed. . .deeply at peace. . .deeply in touch with your sense of well-being. . .from 4 to 3, 3 to 2, and 2 to 1, the elevator continues to descend further and as it does you go deeper and deeper inside yourself, closer and closer to the core of your Being. . .more and more deeply relaxed. . .calmer and more deeply relaxed. . .so calm. . .so peaceful. . .so deeply relaxed. Such a deep sense of well-being.

In just a few moments, you'll find yourself in a safe, peaceful, beautiful, nurturing and loving environment of your own choosing. It is so safe, so peaceful, so beautiful and so loving. You experience such a deep sense of well-being. So now the door of the elevator does open and you do find yourself walking out into a safe, peaceful, beautiful, nurturing and loving environment of your own choosing, your own "inner sanctuary". Look around, walk around this safe, peaceful, beautiful, nurturing and loving inner environment of your own choosing, your "inner sanctuary". Feel the safety, the peace, the beauty, the love of the "inner sanctuary". Sense it, smell it. Touch it. Feel it. So safe, so peaceful, so beautiful, so nurturing and so loving. Your own "inner sanctuary".

CREATION AND MANIFESTATION HOME WORK/PLAY SHEET

A.   FIVE GOALS I'D LIKE TO CREATE IN THE NEXT MONTH:
    1.

    2.

    3.

    4.

    5.

B.   FIVE GOALS I'D LIKE TO CREATE IN THE NEAR FUTURE (3-4 MONTHS):
    1.

    2.

    3.

    4.

    5.

C.   FIVE GOALS I'D LIKE TO CREATE IN THE FUTURE-FUTURE (1 YEAR):
    1.

    2.

    3.

    4.

    5.

D.   FIVE LIFETIME GOALS:
    1.

    2.

    3.

    4.

    5.

AFTER COMPLETING THE EXERCISE FOR EACH TIME PERIOD, CIRCLE THE ONE MOST IMPORTANT GOAL IN EACH PERIOD.

NOTES:

CHAPTER THREE

CREATING POSITIVE, FORGIVING MENTAL ATTITUDES AND POSITIVE, OPTIMISTIC THOUGHTS

A high-powered method for creating positive, forgiving mental attitudes and positive, optimistic thoughts has these twelve steps.

1. **WANTS/GOALS** Clarify the most important wants and goals in your life. Align them with your long-range sense of purpose and vision. Become aware of the relationship between your wants and goals, purpose and vision and core assumptions and beliefs about yourself and your life. It is a powerful law of the mind that whatever you assume and believe, you will perceive. Whatever you assume, believe and conceive, you will perceive and experience; and whatever you assume, believe, conceive, decide and expect, you will

WHATEVER YOU ASSUME, BELIEVE, CONCEIVE, DECIDE AND EXPECT (A + B + C + D + E) YOU WILL PERCEIVE, EXPERIENCE, ACHIEVE AND KNOW (PEAK)

perceive, experience, achieve and know. So you can achieve your wants and goals based on what you choose to assume, believe, conceive, decide and expect. Reflect, for a short time, on what you assume, believe, conceive, decide and expect in your life.

2. **ATTITUDES/THOUGHTS** Your assumptions, beliefs, choices and values about yourself and your life will generate either a positive mental attitude and positive thoughts or a negative mental attitude and negative thoughts. Positive mental attitudes and thoughts in turn generate positive self-talk and positive wants, goals, purposes and visions in life. Negative mental attitudes and thoughts generate negative self-talk. Positive mental attitudes and thoughts generate positive emotions, expectations, achievements and health.

POSITIVE MENTAL ATTITUDES AND THOUGHTS
GENERATE POSITIVE EMOTIONS,
EXPECTATIONS, ACHIEVEMENTS
AND HEALTH

Negative mental attitudes and thoughts generate negative emotions, achievements and health (sickness). Make a list of five of your most positive mental attitudes and thoughts and five of your most negative mental attitudes and thoughts.

3. **SEEDS/WEEDS** Positive mental attitudes and thoughts toward yourself and others are like healthy seeds planted in the garden of your mind. The healthy, positive seeds need to

POSITIVE MENTAL ATTITUDES
ARE LIKE HEALTHY SEEDS

be cultivated with lots of psychological or spiritual sunshine, water and nourishment so they can grow and develop. The weeds need to be identified, uprooted and removed so they don't strangle and destroy the healthy plants (positive mental attitudes and thoughts) expressing themselves when they begin to blossom.

Try this visualization:

- Picture a tiny seed being planted in rich, fertile soil.
- Notice some fertilizer being sprinkled around the seed in order to nurture this tiny little life.
- Visualize the warmth and light of the sun shining down upon the seed and the soil surrounding it, warming and nurturing the little seed.
- Picture the right amount of rain falling upon the soil, giving the earth the perfect amount of moisture to further nurture the seed's growth.
- See the gardener plucking out any weeds surrounding the seed as it begins to grow.
- Imagine the weeds being released from the soil, freeing the seed to grow fuller and stronger.
- Picture the sun and rain and soil nurturing the seed day after day as it sprouts, grows and blossoms.
- Visualize the seed growing into a magnificent and beautiful plant.

4. **CONCENTRATION/FOCUS** What you concentrate on, you absorb. If you concentrate on positive thoughts and at-

WHAT YOU CONCENTRATE ON YOU ABSORB

titudes, you become a positive, uplifting person. If you concentrate on negative judgments toward yourself or other people and negative self-talk and images, you absorb negativity and experience distress. Negative attitudes lead to negative emotions, confusion and upsetting actions. They come from fear and a sense of being separate. Uplifting energy, based on positive attitudes and thoughts, leads to positive emotions, creativity and positive actions and comes from love and joining. What you focus on expands. If you focus on positive mental attitudes, thoughts and energy, they

WHAT YOU FOCUS ON EXPANDS

will expand, grow and be strengthened. If you focus on negative mental attitudes, they will generate distress, expand and grow. You can choose your focus. Reflect on the previous choices you have made in your life and decide whether you want to choose again.

5. **PROJECTOR/MIRROR** The mind is like a projector. Perceptions in your mind are projected out on the world, people

THE MIND IS LIKE A PROJECTOR

and events. Since energy follows thought, energy within you is projected onto the screen of life. The mind is also like a

ENERGY FOLLOWS THOUGHT

mirror. What you see in the world is the reflection of your own state of consciousness. People and events serve as mirrors for your own attitudes and thoughts. Reflect on what

THE MIND IS LIKE A MIRROR

you are projecting and what is being mirrored back to you. Which attitudes, beliefs, thoughts and perceptions would you be willing to change? Make a list.

6. **MAGNET/BRIDGE** The mind is like a magnet. People, events and circumstances are drawn to you in accord with

THE MIND IS LIKE A MAGNET

your attitudes and values. Positive mental attitudes generate positive emotions and draw to you positive events, circumstances, opportunities, challenges and experiences. Negative mental attitudes generate negative emotions and attract negative experiences to you. Consequently, you create events, people, circumstances, opportunities and challenges in your life by your attitudes and thoughts. The mind is also like a bridge. A part of the mind, infinite/creative intelligence, divine/holy spirit or energy actually serves as a

THE MIND IS LIKE A BRIDGE

bridge to either higher or lower consciousness, higher or lower mind. In higher consciousness, there exists higher purpose and vision; while in lower consciousness, there exists lower purpose and vision. Higher consciousness, mind and purpose generate positive, loving mental attitudes and emotions. Lower (ego) consciousness, mind and purpose generate negative or fearful mental attitudes and emotions. You can learn to call upon infinite/creative intelligence to be a bridge to higher mind, higher consciousness and positive, loving attitudes and thoughts.

7. **RESONANCE/ATTUNEMENT** The mind is like a resonator. It will resonate with other like minds like a tuning

THE MIND IS LIKE A RESONATOR

fork. Positive, loving, mental attitudes and thoughts arising from higher consciousness/mind generate positive vibrations and resonate with or are attuned to positive, loving, mental attitudes and vibrations in other minds, because all minds are joined. Negative, fearful mental attitudes and emotions tend to be attuned to all types of negative, fearful mental attitudes and emotions in other minds. In this attunement process, there is an amplification of the dominant thought. Consequently, positive, loving thoughts, attitudes and emotions are amplified. The same is true of negative attitudes and emotions. You can choose to resonate with and amplify positive or negative attitudes and emotions.

8. **RESPONSIBILITY/POWER** You are responsible for your attitudes, beliefs, values, thoughts and energy. You learn to develop positive or negative mental attitudes. No one else is

YOU ARE RESPONSIBLE FOR YOUR ATTITUDES, THOUGHTS AND ENERGY

responsible for your thoughts, attitudes, values and beliefs except you. You can learn to change your negative mental attitudes and thoughts into positive ones. Furthermore, you can call upon an inner power to help you. This infinite/creative intelligence is the powerful force that serves as your bridge and guide to higher consciousness and higher mind. It can help you learn how to develop more positive, loving mental attitudes and thoughts. Close your eyes. Relax. Breathe deeply for a few minutes. Then ask this inner power to guide you.

9. **FORGIVENESS/HEALING** With practice and inner guidance, you can learn to develop more positive, loving mental attitudes. First, learn to let go of negative mental attitudes and judgments of yourself and others. This process of letting go is referred to as forgiveness. It requires you to

THE PROCESS OF LETTING GO IS REFERRED TO AS FORGIVENESS

take responsibility for the creation of the negative attitudes and thoughts that you hold toward yourself and others. They generate anger, hurt, pain, guilt, bitterness, rejection, depression, fear, illness and disharmony in relationships. By releasing this negative mind set, you will free yourself to experience increasing amounts of positive, loving, enthusiastic, joyful and peaceful emotions. You will in turn activate a profound healing process which will take place on the level of body, mind, emotions, relationships and spirit. You can ask for help from this inner power in the letting go, forgiveness, and healing process. As the process occurs, you will find yourself more aligned with your true Self and more able to experience the positive feelings and creativity of higher consciousness/higher mind.

10. **OPTIMISM/LIGHT** As you learn how to forgive yourself and others, you will let go of a great deal of negative emotion. The positive emotion that is released will generate an increasing amount of optimism in your life. You will find

THE POSITIVE EMOTION RELEASED
WILL GENERATE OPTIMISM

yourself consistently looking on the bright side of things. You will have more energy to achieve your goals; your relationships will improve dramatically; your health will improve; and you will develop a more positive sense of purpose and vision in life. You will increasingly see the goodness, worthiness, love, joy and peace in yourself and other people instead of the darkness. You will discover you have an inner light aligned with the core of your Being, your Higher Self, and aligned with the essence or core of everyone's Being or Self. Take a few moments to sit quietly. Reflect on ways in which you can experience more optimism and light.

11. **GIVE/RECEIVE** As you give, so you receive. Expressing positive mental attitudes will generate positive feelings and

AS YOU GIVE, SO YOU RECEIVE

actions on your part. These positive feelings and actions will in turn generate positive feelings and actions from other people directed toward you. In particular, letting go of negative, blaming and judgmental attitudes and replacing them with positive, loving, forgiving attitudes will markedly improve your relationships. In addition, because of the magnet and resonance effect of positive attitudes, thoughts and actions, you will draw positive people, actions, circumstances and events toward you. Even more important, however, is the immediate benefits you will receive from sharing (giving) positive mental attitudes in a loving, caring, compassionate way. You will immediately experience (receive) the benefits because you will feel good; you will feel compassionate and loving inside. You will immediately experience more peace of mind, joy, self-worth and light. Visualize yourself offering love and forgiveness to another person. See and feel yourself receiving the positive effects of your giving.

12. **SOW/REAP** As you sow, so you reap. What you give to others, you give to yourself. These are basic, universal laws.

WHAT YOU GIVE TO OTHERS
YOU GIVE TO YOURSELF

The feedback effect may be immediate or it may be delayed. It will occur in direct proportion to the energy sent out. The same goes for service performed. Loving and creative service will be rewarded in one form or another; e.g., success, recognition, material benefits, enhanced business. More important, however, is knowing that it will give you a greater sense of contribution in life and a greater feeling of peace, love, joy, self-worth and well-being. Close your eyes and picture yourself sowing positive attitudes, thoughts, feelings and actions. Then picture yourself reaping the fruits of your actions, both immediately and over time.

Read and reread the 12 steps to creating positive, forgiving mental attitudes and positive, optimistic thoughts. Then practice the ideas and processes. Gradually, day by day, and sometimes dramatically, you will discover your well-being greatly enhanced and a transformation taking place in the quality of your life.

Mary called me in a highly distressed state after she saw an article about my work in The Philadelphia Inquirer. We first met a week later at one of our seminars. She was in her middle 40's with two children. Confused, depressed, anxious and directionless were probably the most appropriate terms to describe Mary's mental and emotional state at the time. Her facial expression was gloomy, constricted and tense. During the weekend seminar, she allowed herself to first experience and then release a tremendous amount of anger she held toward her elderly, sick father. She told the group that every time she thought of him, hate welled up within her. She worked diligently with the forgiveness exercises, letting go of expectations, judgments and hurt feelings. Mary stopped making her father wrong and herself right for perceived critical comments by her father. She stopped complaining about him for his apparent indifference to her in favor of her stepmother, Joan. She realized she was just seeking the love of which she felt deprived. Eventually, Mary realized she didn't love herself sufficiently and so was seeking the love from her father that she wasn't giving to herself. She was able to re-perceive her father's fault-finding behavior as coming from fear and as a call for love. In the safe, supportive and nurturing context of the seminar, Mary received a great deal of love from other participants and gave love as well. She cried profusely as she shared her hurt, rage and fears. She was held and warmly hugged by other group members.

At the end of the seminar, Mary was elated. She was smiling, cheerful, loving and peaceful. Like many participants, her whole demeanor, facial expression and outlook was changed, uplifted, radiant and glowing. With a new, positive attitude, she immediately contacted her father. Mary visited with him for the first time in over a year. At first cautious, he eventually welcomed her with open arms and they both cried together. In the weeks and months to come, the healing of the relationship deepened.

Mary came to see me for individual therapy sessions follow-ing the seminar to work on fears of losing her hair (which she wasn't), some conflicts with her daughter, and possible career aspirations (she hadn't been employed in ten years). Together we set specific goals for her (self-esteem, relaxation, mother-daughter and career) and I helped her visualize the attainment of these goals. We worked on enhancing her self-esteem by letting go of self-criticisms she had learned from her (deceased) mother. By learning how to forgive her mother and herself, her relations with her daughter improved. She released judgments and expec-tations. Gradually she took on a part-time job as a secretary. Six months later she was starting her own specialty clothing business with a friend of hers. Mary had dramatically turned her life around in nine months. She was happy, peaceful and enthusias-tic. She had healed several relationships, both with the living (father, daughter, self), and with the deceased (mother).

Barbara was 42 years old, married with two children. When she came to see me, she was extremely depressed and guilt-rid-den over a five month affair that had just ended. She felt rejected by her lover, Sam, whom she had met at work, and was angry at herself for not breaking the relationship off earlier. Barbara was also angry at her husband, Bob, for being so insensitive to her and being a tyrant, and was generally confused and distraught. For the first three or four months of her affair, which was really out of character for her, she felt sexually excited, like a teenager awak-ening to her sexuality for the first time. Now she was remorseful and bitter. Moreover, her son Bill was having serious difficulties in school (grades dropping, peer relationship problems) "coin-cidentally" during this same five month period of time. Barbara had also become increasingly unhappy with her bookkeeping job where she met her lover, Sam, five years her junior.

In the first few weeks, Barbara anxiously called me several times, distraught over her son, an argument with her husband, or a phone call from Sam. She would schedule emergency sessions with me to cope with her fear, hurt, anger, and guilt. When she came in she would be tearful and distressed and complain to me about one of the males in her life. Later I found out that both her father and brother-in-law had affairs years earlier for which she always bitterly resented them. She had blamed them and swore that nothing like that could or would ever happen to her.

To start, I taught Barbara the relaxation, visualization and goal-setting process. Many of the early sessions, however, were spent on helping her to first forgive herself; i.e., let go of her intense self-judgment, then forgive her ex-lover, and finally forgive her husband. We worked with the forgiveness imagery exercise. Both her husband and 12 year old son attended one of the 14 sessions we held together. Barbara's emotions were very volatile at first. Early sessions were something like a confessional. I would support Barbara in seeing herself as free of guilt and sin and encourage her to love and forgive herself. She would then repeat positive affirmations such as, "I am innocent, healed and lovable." I also helped her to relax, get clear about what she wanted (her goals) and encouraged her to work on improving her relationship with her husband. Gradually, Barbara calmed down, forgave herself, released many negative self-judgments, enhanced her self-worth, joined her husband in some physical self-improvement classes, brought some emotional closure to the affair and quit her job.

I liked Barbara very much and was delighted to see that her relationship with her husband improved, her son's school problems cleared up, and that she decided she wanted to go back to school so she could switch the direction of her career. Overall, Barbara's depression, guilt and stress dropped markedly and her self-esteem improved substantially. She was a much happier and more self-confident woman. I have occasionally spoken to her on the phone since then. She is doing well, coping with the daily challenges of life and eager to pursue her education.

ATTITUDE/THOUGHT
HOME WORK/PLAY SHEET

A.   FIVE NAMES OF PEOPLE I NEED OR WANT TO FORGIVE:
     1.

     2.

     3.

     4.

     5.

B.   FIVE NAMES OF PEOPLE I'D LIKE TO ASK FORGIVENESS FROM:
     1.

     2.

     3.

     4.

     5.

C.   FIVE QUALITIES (THOUGHTS, FEELINGS, ATTITUDES, BEHAVIORS)
     I NEED TO FORGIVE MYSELF FOR:
     1.

     2.

     3.

     4.

     5.

YOU CAN ADD MORE THAN FIVE PEOPLE OR QUALITIES, OR LIST LESS
THAN FIVE, DEPENDING ON YOUR LIFE EXPERIENCE AND CIR-
CUMSTANCES. IT IS HELPFUL, HOWEVER, TO TRY AND LIST ALL FIVE
FOR EACH GROUP.

FORGIVENESS EXERCISES

A. FORGIVING ANOTHER

Part I: Close your eyes. Breathe deeply. Relax. Allow your attention to focus on your breath. Continue to breathe slowly and deeply. Breathing in and out slowly and deeply. . . .slowly and deeply. Concentrate on your breath as it rises and falls. . . .slowly and deeply. . . .Breathing in and out. Focusing on the breath. Now repeat the word "calm" on the in-breath and "relax" on the out-breath. "Calm" on the in-breath, "relax" on the out-breath, silently to yourself. Breathing in "calm", "breathing out "relax", slowly and deeply, "calm" and "relax", slowly and deeply, "calm" and "relax". Focusing on the breath, slowly and deeply, "calm" and "relax". Now ask the creative/infinite intelligence, the divine/holy spirit to help you with the forgiveness process.

Part II: Think of someone you dislike, actively despise or hate, someone you are angry at, or just someone you are very uncomfortable with. Say to that person, "I forgive you." "I forgive you for anything you may have done consciously or unconsciously, intentionally or unintentionally, that I believe has caused me pain or hurt. I forgive you for any thought, feeling, act or deed that you have done. I forgive you." Allow you heart to open to this person you have judged, you have condemned. Open your mind to doubt.

Opening. . .softening. . .softening. . .opening. . .releasing. . .letting go. Now continue to breathe in and out slowly and deeply. "Calm" and "relax"; "relax" and "calm". Opening, opening, more. Softening, softening more, releasing, releasing more, letting go, letting go more. "I forgive you (mention that person's name). I forgive you for the hurt I perceive or I think you may have caused me. I am open to doubt. Perhaps it was just a mistake, an error. I forgive you. I release you. I release me from the pain, the hurt, the fear, the sadness, the incredible anger. I let it go, now. . .opening, softening, softening, opening, releasing, letting go. Breathing slowly and deeply, deeply and slowly. I allow myself to see your innocence. I allow myself to feel your pain, your hurt. I allow myself to touch your heart and be touched by your heart. It is so hard to keep oneself out of another's heart. Feel your heart opening and touching this person's heart.

Opening, softening, touching, releasing, letting go. I forgive you for anything you did that caused me hurt or pain. I see your innocence. I see your light. I see my innocence. I see your worth. I see my worth. I release you of all judgments I have made against you. I let go of all expectations I had for you. I release all judgments or expectations I have made against myself. I release the hurt, the pain, the anger, the fear, the darkness. I forgive you. I release you. I forgive me. I am at peace. I am at peace. Opening, softening, releasing, letting go. Breathing slowly and deeply. Calm and relaxed. Calm and relaxed. At peace. At peace.

B. ASKING FOR FORGIVENESS FROM ANOTHER

Repeat Part I. And once again ask the creative/infinite intelligence, the divine/holy spirit or energy to help you. (Select a person from whom you want to ask forgiveness.)

Part II: "I ask your forgiveness for anything I may have done, consciously or unconsciously, intentionally or unintentionally, that I believe has caused you hurt, pain or suffering. I ask your forgiveness. I ask your forgiveness (fill in the person's name) for any thought, feeling, word, gesture, or behavior that I did or contemplated doing that I perceive injured you in any way. I ask your forgiveness for any condemnation, judgment, complaints, gossip, expectations or deeds I may have done that I think has caused you any distress or guilt or pain. I ask your forgiveness. Opening, letting go, letting go, releasing. I ask your forgiveness! I ask your forgiveness. I ask your forgiveness.

Breathing slowly and deeply, deeply and slowly. "Calm" and "relax". "Relax" and "calm". I release any judgment, any attack thoughts, condemnation or anger I may have thought or said or written toward you. I release them. I let them go and I ask your forgiveness. Softening, opening, releasing, letting go. I allow my mind to open, to trust. I allow my heart to open to your heart; I allow myself to be touched by your heart. I allow myself to feel your compassion, your love. Opening, softening, releasing, letting go. I ask your forgiveness. Touching your heart, feeling your compassion, experiencing your love. Opening, softening. Breathing, slowly and deeply, calm and relax. Calm and relax. Peace and love. Peace and love.

C. SELF-FORGIVENESS

Repeat Part I. Once again ask the creative/infinite intelligence, the divine/holy spirit or energy to help you to forgive yourself.

Part II: Self-forgiveness. Forgiving oneself. Repeat to yourself, "I forgive me for anything I think I did consciously or unconsciously, intentionally or unintentionally that caused me or anyone else hurt or pain. Say to yourself, "I forgive me (use your own name). I forgive myself for any feeling, attitude or judgment I may have contemplated, held or experienced that I perceive caused me or anyone else anger, guilt, sadness, or pain. I forgive me. Opening, softening, softening, opening. I forgive me (use your name) for any condemnation, criticism, or attack thoughts that I used against myself or another to diminish, demoralize or depress myself or another. I forgive me. I forgive me. I forgive me. Releasing, letting go, letting go, releasing. I forgive me for any self-hatred, anger or guilt that I used to devalue myself or undermine my self-worth or my self-respect. I forgive me. I forgive me for any thought, act, behavior or deed that I believe hurt or injured or caused distress to anyone else or to myself. I forgive me."

"Softening, opening, opening, softening. Releasing all doubt, all judgment, all 'shoulds', all negativity, all expectations. Letting go of all pain, all the sorrow, all the hurt, all the fear, all the anger. I forgive me and I accept me." Allow yourself to perceive your innocence. Allow yourself to see your essential worth. Allow yourself to experience your inner light and love. Say, "I forgive me," to yourself. Allow your heart to open to you. Opening, softening, softening, opening. Allow yourself to feel compassion for you. Touch your hurt with your incredible compassion. Touch your heart with your

kindness and understanding. Opening, softening. Forgive yourself. Touch yourself. Love yourself. Allow yourself to be loved. Allow yourself to love yourself.

Feel the incredible love you have for yourself. Feel your innocence. Feel your worth. See your incredible light and inner beauty. Feel your love for you. Relax and calm. Love and peace. Allow yourself to love yourself. Deeply, unconditionally love yourself. Ask the creative/infinite intelligence, the divine/holy spirit or energy to help you to love yourself. Deeply. Profoundly. Unconditionally. Allow yourself to love yourself. Deeply, unconditionally love yourself. Say to yourself, "I love you. You are loved. I love you. You are loved. I love you." Be at peace.

CHAPTER FOUR

LEARNING HOW TO RE-PERCEIVE AND REFRAME THE EVENTS, SITUATIONS, CIRCUMSTANCES AND PEOPLE IN YOUR LIFE

You can learn how to re-perceive and reframe the events, situations and people in your life in a more useful, helpful and constructive way.

1. **ATTITUDES/THOUGHTS** Mental attitudes and thoughts generate energy. This energy becomes projected by the mind onto the screen of the world. It is then reflected back to you, like a mirror, in the attitudes, feelings and behavior of other people as they interact with you. Since your mind is like a magnet, it will also draw to you positive or negative events, circumstances and people, depending on whether you hold positive or negative mental attitudes, thoughts and beliefs. Your mind is also a bridge to higher or lower consciousness, higher or lower mind, mediated by infinite/creative intelligence. If you are attuned to higher consciousness, higher mind, your positive, loving and forgiving attitudes, thoughts

*YOUR MIND IS A BRIDGE TO HIGHER OR
LOWER CONCIOUSNESS, HIGHER OR
LOWER MIND, MEDIATED BY
INFINITE/CREATIVE INTELLIGENCE*

and energy will resonate with and be amplified by the positive energy of others. What you give is what you receive. What you sow is what you reap. What you focus on expands. Reflect for a few moments and then focus on experiencing and sending positive, loving energy to others.

2. **RE-PERCEIVE/REFRAME** Every action can be perceived through the lens of higher mind, higher consciousness or lower mind, lower (ego) consciousness. Every situation that may initially be perceived with a dark frame around it can be re-perceived with a light one. Every situation that may at first appear unfortunate or unpleasant can be re-perceived or re-

*EVERY SITUATION THAT MAY INITIALLY BE
PERCEIVED WITH A DARK FRAME AROUND IT
CAN BE RE-PERCEIVED WITH A LIGHT ONE*

framed as an opportunity to learn a lesson. When we perceive another's behavior in a way that we find distressing, we can learn to separate the behavior from the intention behind it. There is always a positive intention behind behavior, no matter how upsetting it may appear. You can learn, for example, to perceive that a behavior which appears to be attacking is actually covering up fear, and that fear is always a call for help and a call for love; or that a so-called failure, disappointment, or illness is an opportunity to change directions, strategies or life's purpose.

3. **IMAGES/PICTURES** You see the world, relationships and yourself through images you created. These images in turn

are generated by your thoughts and attitudes which in turn arise from your core values, beliefs and expectations. They are often emotionally charged and connote feelings and judgments of being loved or unloved, worthy or unworthy, successful or unsuccessful, healthy or ill, competent or incompetent, good or bad, wealthy or poor, strong or weak,

YOU SEE THE WORLD AND YOURSELF
THROUGH IMAGES YOU CREATED

peaceful or fearful. Throughout your life you will engage in activities, behaviors and relationships that will attempt to either defend against or seek to change these emotion-backed images. You will often seek relationships and circumstances in the hope that they will meet your needs to experience more love, worthiness, success, health, competence, wealth, strength, goodness and peace. Close your eyes and relax. Take some slow deep breaths. Reflect on the images and pictures you have created in your mind about yourself, your relations, and your life.

4. **SUBCONSCIOUS/SUPERCONSCIOUS** Your conscious mind is usually made up of ego-based attitudes and images arising from lower consciousness. Your subconscious mind, on the other hand, stores emotion-backed images from the past. There are two levels of the subconscious mind. At the first level are images, thoughts, memories and feelings of which you are not consciously aware until you focus your mind in that direction. In the second, deeper level of the subconscious mind (the unconscious), are images, thoughts, attitudes, beliefs and emotions that are out of your awareness. You do not have easy access to them even when you focus your mind in that direction. There is an even deeper, more powerful, wiser and spiritual level, the superconscious mind, where truths of higher consciousness, higher mind and the inner Self reside. Conflicting images, thoughts, attitudes,

beliefs, values and emotions frequently reside in the two levels of the subconscious mind or in the conscious mind. However, the superconscious mind is always unified around basic truths, purposes and goals.

THE SUPERCONSCIOUS MIND IS UNIFIED AROUND BASIC TRUTHS

5. **MEDIATOR/GUIDE** Within the mind there is a mediator between the fearful thoughts of the "ego" which resides in the conscious, subconscious and unconscious mind and the higher, superconscious mind. Think of this mediator as infinite/creative intelligence or divine/holy spirit or energy.

THE MEDIATOR IS INFINITE/CREATIVE INTELLIGENCE OR DIVINE/HOLY SPIRIT

Call upon the mediator and it will guide you to re-perceive and reframe the way you perceive yourself, your relationships and your life. It will serve as an inner teacher or voice, gently pointing you back in the direction of the love and wisdom of the superconscious mind and the truths of higher consciousness. The guide will assist you in resolving contradictions among attitudes, thoughts, beliefs, values, images and feelings.

6. **SILENCE/MEDITATION** By silencing your mind and going inside, make contact with your inner guide, teacher, voice or mediator. Find a quiet place. Close your eyes and engage in slow, deep breathing. Deepen this experience by entering a state of meditation. To do this you may want to focus on the breath and repeat a particular number, phrase, mantra, name or prayer. In the silence, in meditation, with the assistance of your inner guide, contemplate at a deeper level how you can re-perceive and reframe situations and problems so that you can perceive them through the positive, loving lens of superconscious mind. You can also seek for deeper resolutions

of the internal contradictions within you. In the meditative silence, begin to realign your conscious, subconscious, unconscious and superconscious mind. Close your eyes now, breathe deeply, meditate and listen within for your inner guide, voice or teacher.

7. **REPROGRAM/REDIRECT** Learn to reprogram and redirect the attitudes, images and thoughts in your conscious

YOU CAN LEARN TO REPROGRAM AND
REDIRECT YOUR MIND

and subconscious mind. By doing so, you will not only be able to re-perceive and reframe current situations, events and relations, but also earlier life experiences with family members, teachers and friends. You can do this by entering into a meditative space while asking for the assistance of your source of creative intelligence, then mentally turning the clock back to an earlier time when you experienced emotional distress. One of the capacities of the inner guide is the ability to delete, edit and erase earlier life scripts. Imagine that your subconscious mind has an endless series of inner videotapes. Replay earlier life scripts on this inner video screen; re-perceive and reframe them from the perspective of the superconscious mind and then erase, delete or edit them. For example, angry, hurtful, fearful exchanges with relatives or teachers can be edited into loving, forgiving, peaceful exchanges. This will contribute greatly to reprogramming and redirecting your mind in a healthy way. Try it now.

8. **AFFIRMATIONS/INSPIRATIONS** After re-perceiving and reframing present and past experiences, you can use positive affirmations to help you reprogram your current conscious, negative, mental attitudes, images and self-talk into positive ones. Positive affirmations are positive statements you af-

firm and repeat over and over about yourself, your relationships and any aspect of your life. If done correctly, these positive affirmations can be a source of great inspiration to

*POSITIVE AFFIRMATIONS ARE POSITIVE
STATEMENTS YOU AFFIRM OVER AND OVER
ABOUT YOURSELF, YOUR RELATIONSHIPS
AND YOUR LIFE*

you. For example, you could say "I am forgiving, loving, joyful and peaceful"; "I have a wonderful, sensitive, loving man or woman in my life"; or "I am getting stronger and stronger, healthier and healthier, more and more successful every day"; or "I am competent, worthwhile, happy and creative." It is helpful to repeat affirmations for 10-15 minutes a day while looking in the mirror, or write them down for 10-15 minutes per day, or listen to them on a homemade audiocassette. In order to inspire yourself, repeat them silently or out loud throughout the day. Try writing and repeating some positive affirmations now.

9. **KNOWLEDGE/WISDOM** Learn how to reframe and reperceive people, situations, events, and even your own self-image, in a more useful, helpful way. By accessing the knowledge of the superconscious mind with your inner guidance, you can begin to see yourself and your life differently. Utilize positive affirmations in ways that will align you with your higher purpose and vision and resorate with the core of your Being, the inner light within you. See others in a different way, as either communicating love, appreciation, respect, value and acceptance, or as asking for them.

*SEE OTHERS AS COMMUNICATING LOVE
OR ASKING FOR LOVE*

Access the wisdom of infinite/creative intelligence in helping you develop more constructive ways in which to relate. Begin to see new opportunities and options. Allow yourself to feel more grateful for what you have already received.

10. **TEACHINGS/LESSONS** Every situation, event, circumstance and interaction in your life can be re-perceived and reframed as a lesson in the schoolroom of life. If you are open to receiving the wisdom that your experiences have to offer, your life will be an ongoing course with a curriculum made of the highest teachings. By asking for inner guidance, you will discover that infinite/creative intelligence will be a great support. Every interaction in your life can be thought of as a teaching lesson designed specifically for you. Every

EVERY INTERACTION IN YOUR LIFE
CAN BE THOUGHT OF AS A TEACHING LESSON
DESIGNED SPECIFICALLY FOR YOU

person you speak with can be perceived as your teacher. Look with an open mind and heart for the positive lesson. You can heal yourself and your relationships, discover new possibilities for growth or success, and transform the quality of your life. Reflect on how you can do this now.

11. **INCREASE/STRENGTHEN** Every time you communicate an idea, belief, thought or attitude to another person, you are a teacher and the other person is a student. What you teach, you learn. What you teach others, you increase in yourself. If you teach positive and uplifting thoughts, that is what will be increased in your thinking. Since positive beliefs and thoughts generate positive energy, you will be increasing positive, loving energy in yourself. What you communicate, you teach; what you teach, you focus on; what you focus on, expands; what expands, you strengthen. The same is true of

WHAT YOU COMMUNICATE, YOU TEACH;
WHAT YOU TEACH, YOU FOCUS ON

WHAT YOU FOCUS ON, EXPANDS;
WHAT EXPANDS, YOU STRENGTHEN

negative beliefs and thoughts. The superconscious mind is made up of loving, joyful, peaceful thoughts and feelings. With the assistance of infinite/creative intelligence, you can learn how to increase and strengthen your awareness of positive, uplifting thoughts and energy.

12. **JOINING/CONNECTING** You can discover that the superconscious mind is made up of positive, loving, vibrational energy of higher consciousness. This energy, when shared, extends itself to others and joins with them. In fact, at the level of the superconscious mind, all minds are already joined. The more you share positive thoughts, attitudes and

AT THE LEVEL OF THE SUPERCONSCIOUS MIND
ALL MINDS ARE ALREADY JOINED

feelings with others, the more you will join with them. This joining and sharing will increase, strengthen and amplify positive and healing energy. You will be connecting with another at a deep and profound level of consciousness, your

SHARING WILL INCREASE, STRENGTHEN
AND AMPLIFY HEALING ENERGY

truest level of Being, your higher Self, your inner Light. Experience upliftment and inspiration from contacting this core of your Being. Allow infinite/creative intelligence to help you. Close your eyes. Breathe deeply. Relax. Visualize yourself sending and receiving positive, optimistic, loving, forgiving, healing thoughts to and from another. Feel yourself joined and connected to this person at a deep, profound level.

Paul came to the weekend seminar eager to further his personal, relational, career and spiritual growth. He was 38 years old, separated from his wife, and a very friendly person. Yet underneath this outer surface warmth was an intense hatred and hurt in relation to his father. I was initially surprised, given the intensity of his anger and the vivid description of abuse, humiliation and rejection he gave, that Paul's father had been dead for 12 years. Paul's disguised calls for love to redress the hurt and fear were very obvious. He did, however, hold onto the erroneous belief that nothing could be done about the situation because his father was dead. I gently challenge clients or seminar participants when they say "I can't change my thoughts, feelings or behaviors", because "I can't", creates a mental and emotional trap that imprisons them.

So, sensing that he would be willing and able to do it, I asked Paul to roleplay a dialogue with his father in front of the group, even though he had never shared his feelings with his father when he was alive. I asked one of my assistants to roleplay Paul's father, first as Paul portrayed him, and then as Paul always wanted him to be; the loving, caring father who listened to and accepted Paul's thoughts and feelings. Within this supportive group setting, Paul felt free to cry. He was hugged lovingly, first by the assistant roleplaying Paul's father, and then by everyone in the group.

The second day of the seminar had an even more powerful effect on Paul. During the forgiveness exercises, he released just about all of his negativity, anger, hurt and disappointment toward his father. At the same time, he released much of his self-hatred, self-criticism and guilt toward himself; i.e., he began to forgive himself and to love himself as he forgave his father and began to learn to accept, appreciate and love both his father and himself. Again, Paul wept. Again, the group was lovingly supportive and nurturing and hugged him. Paul reported feeling cleansed, healed and loved. We were all moved as we experienced the healing of painful memories and relationships.

A week later, I received a letter from Paul, excerpts of which follow:

Dear Phil,

I'm taking advantage of your generous offer to let us write you. I need to tell you just how special that weekend was for me. Many fabulous breakthroughs have happened for me since your seminar. There have been a lot of "incomplete's" in my life. I have been terrified of meeting dozens of people since I moved back into this area. Three weeks ago, I met an "old friend". I felt I had to tell him that I was developing a real estate business. Two days ago, I met another ex-co-worker. I was tempted to use the same story (real estate is a dream of mine), but I stopped myself. I realized that he had the same job. I wasn't trying to impress him; I was easing a burden of guilt that I laid on myself.

I was an EMT/Paramedic for five years. When I was "just" an EMT, the responsibility of death wasn't mine. But as a paramedic, I took the burden on myself. I worked on three people who had been dead for over ten minutes. We did CPR on them and all the usual rescue stuff. I felt my incompetence killed them. I walked away from the squad, not even stopping to turn in my keys! For years I've been saying, "If I had been better trained. . ." Yesterday, I saw it from their point of view. "Lots of people have seen too much death and have cracked." Yesterday I forgave myself.

I've been paralyzed all my life; Never able to make a decision. "What if I make the wrong choice;" You and Carol (a friend who attended the seminar) taught me that I can choose today and change my mind tomorrow if I don't like it. So on Thursday, I told my manager and ex-manager that I want to be an assistant manager for the store. They were very positive about the idea. . .I also believe I will change the group with which I am involved to fulfill my commitment to my Higher Power. . .I would like to re-emphasize that I would love to take your advanced seminar and also be an assistant for you at some time in the future.

Thank you for everything. "Phil, we are perfect!"

Love and Peace,

Paul

Donna was 42 years old, married with two teenage children when she first attended one of our introductory evening seminars. I remember she had a lot of questions to ask, both perceptive and challenging. She was unclear as to the direction of her life, troubled by her marriage, and searching openly for answers. The basic weekend seminar was a powerful one for her, but not as profound as the three day advanced seminar she took some months later. She had been constantly prodding her 43 year old husband, Ted, to take the basic seminar and finally he did. Ted was able to contact a tremendous amount of joy, love and generosity within himself following the seminar. He was high from inner ecstasy and exuberant for weeks afterward. He organized an unusual and uplifting follow-up for the participants at his photography studio. There he took incredibly beautiful photographs of the seminar participants and later presented them as gifts of love to each person, for which we will always be grateful.

Somewhat to my surprise, Ted and Donna, largely at Ted's initiative, separated soon after that. I recall that I had to release some expectations, judgments and even disappointment when I heard the news. Nevertheless, they both attended a more advanced three day seminar, "Teach Only Love", together some weeks later. In that seminar, Ted had a remarkable healing experience. During a guided imagery process, he found himself reliving a Vietnam War occurrence. He saw himself flying a plane over a small lake when he sighted a Viet Cong soldier in a boat. His instructions at the time were to bomb and destroy any "enemy" soldier. Ted originally saw the Viet Cong soldier reaching up in the air with outstretched arms pleading with him in terror not to drop the bomb. He did drop the bomb, however, killing the so-called "enemy". Ted later said he had repressed the memory but felt intense guilt at what had happened. During the seminar, he relived the entire experience but this time as he flew over the Viet Cong soldier, he saw him as his "brother", looking up at him with forgiving eyes and radiating unconditional love and acceptance. Ted said at that moment, the guilt dissolved; he felt unconditional love for the soldier; he forgave himself for the killing; and he loved himself unconditionally. He cried very hard for a long time. When the tears finally stopped, he reported a deep peace and acceptance unlike anything he had ever experienced before. He said he felt profoundly cleansed.

Meanwhile, Donna was having her own deeply moving experience of unconditional love and acceptance during the seminar: she was able to totally accept Ted, even though he did not choose to reunite with her. She was able to totally release judgments of herself and Ted, to forgive both of them, and to be at peace. She reported feeling one with God during the experience as if she had come home to her truest nature, Self or Being.

After the seminar, Donna and Ted continued to move further apart physically and eventually divorced amicably. Ted briefly pursued some therapy and extensively became involved in further personal growth work. Every time I saw him he look absolutely joyful. He began to volunteer a lot of his time serving others while Donna pursued her interest in healing, took training seminars in another state, and moved with her children into a healing community. She met another man and, with his assistance, eventually started her own healing center. Ted's career flourished, he dated, and continued to grow in very positive ways.

RE-PERCEIVE/REFRAME
HOME WORK/PLAY SHEET

LIST TEN EVENTS, SITUATIONS, CIRCUMSTANCES, OR PEOPLE IN YOUR LIFE (PAST OR PRESENT) THAT YOU WANT TO LEARN HOW TO RE-PERCEIVE AND REFRAME:

1.

2.

3.

4.

5.

6.

7.

8.

9.

10.

AFTER LISTING THE TEN, GO BACK OVER THE LIST AND JOT DOWN SOME IDEAS ON HOW YOU CAN RE-PERCEIVE AND REFRAME THEM. (YOU MAY WANT TO CLOSE YOUR EYES BRIEFLY AND ASK THE CREATIVE/INFINITE INTELLIGENCE, THE DIVINE/HOLY SPIRIT OR ENERGY WITHIN HOW YOU CAN DO THIS.)

NOTES:

CHAPTER FIVE

GENERATING CREATIVE ALTERNATIVES AND POSSIBILITIES IN LIFE

There are twelve guidelines for generating creative alternatives and possibilities for solving problems in life.

1. **RE-PERCEIVE/REFRAME** You can learn to re-perceive and reframe situations, events, and people in a more positive, constructive and uplifting way. What you previously perceived through a dark lens or frame can be seen, with the help of infinite/creative intelligence, through a light lens. You can learn to look for the lessons inherent in every situation, and, in the process, transform unpleasant, unfortunate appearing experiences into healing, positive ones. By accessing your superconscious mind, utilizing positive affirmations to inspire you, editing painful memories from the past and by reprogramming and redirecting your mind in a positive direction, you can discover great wisdom and profound teachings in all your experiences. What you communicate,

YOU CAN DISCOVER GREAT WISDOM AND
PROFOUND TEACHINGS

you teach. What you teach, you focus on. What you focus on, expands. What expands, you strengthen. Reflect on what you have thought, learned, communicated, taught, focused on and strengthened from previous life experiences. Remember, at a deep level, all minds are joined. You are not alone in experiencing the effects of your thoughts and communications.

2. **ALTERNATIVES/POSSIBILITIES** For every perceived problem, there are many alternative and possible solutions, though unseen at the moment. In fact, a solution is always inherent within every problem. When perceiving a problem,

A SOLUTION IS ALWAYS INHERENT
WITHIN EVERY PROBLEM

you can learn to welcome it by saying, "A problem, that's good". When problems are welcomed, you will see them as signals to use your creativity and imagination. You will immediately find yourself thinking in terms of generating new options, alternatives and possibilities. Your mind will explore, discover and eventually evaluate creative avenues for resolving the perceived problem. You will be in a receptive frame of mind. Close your eyes. Relax and breathe deeply for 1-2 minutes. Allow your mind to search for new, creative alternatives and possibilities to perceived problems.

3. **CHALLENGES/OPPORTUNITIES** When you allow yourself to welcome perceived difficulties, you see them as challenges requiring creative solutions and opportunities for change, growth and expansion. You can let go of (and forgive) the past, live in the present, and look positively toward the future. What you previously perceived as a stumbling block, you can now perceive as a stepping stone. The previously perceived obstacle or detriment can now be perceived as a gift. Your self-talk can inspire rather than depress

WHAT YOU PREVIOUSLY PERCEIVED
AS A STUMBLING BLOCK OR OBSTACLE,
YOU CAN NOW PERCEIVE
AS A STEPPING STONE OR GIFT

you. Your previous **"I can't"** (think, do, feel, or change something), can change to **"I can"** (think, do, feel or change something). **"Winners"** come in **"cans"** and **"losers"** come in **"can'ts"**. Reflect for a while on how you can turn stumbling blocks into stepping stones and see problems and difficulties as challenges and opportunities. Write down some of your ideas.

4. **ADVANTAGES/GAINS** Inherent in every perceived disadvantage is an equal or greater advantage. Inherent in every perceived loss is an equal or greater gain. Inherent in every perceived cost is an equal or greater benefit. Inherent in

INHERENT IN EVERY PERCEIVED COST
IS AN EQUAL OR GREATER GAIN
INHERENT IN EVERY PERCEIVED FAILURE
IS THE SEED OF A GREATER SUCCESS

every perceived failure is the seed of a greater success. Reread the above statements over and over again. You can transform your thinking and your consciousness from negative and discouraged to positive and inspired. You can create new life-affirming wants and goals consistent with your purpose and vision in life. You can make constructive choices and decisions. You can create powerful dreams and desires, aligned with the core of your Being, your true inner Self. You can visualize attaining these goals and dreams. You can discover the advantages and successes inherent within the perceived disadvantages and failures. You can do it now. Write down three creative possibilities, alternatives and opportunities available to you in your life now. Choose to explore them.

5. **PROBLEMS/SOLUTIONS** Inherent in every problem is the solution. Inherent in every grievance is the opportunity for forgiveness. Inherent in every illness is the opportunity for healing. Inherent in every conflict is the opportunity for peace. What do each of the above statements have in common? Every problem, grievance, illness and conflict arises from the lower consciousness of the "ego" which is based on a sense of feeling separate from your true Self, the core of

EVERY PROBLEM ARISES FROM A SENSE
OF FEELING SEPARATE
EVERY SOLUTION ARISES FROM JOINING

your Being. Every solution arises from joining with the higher (super) consciousness of your true Self. All sense of separateness is based on perceiving yourself and other people in bodies (lower consciousness). All sense of joining is based on perceiving yourself and other people as spirit (higher consciousness). Every perceived problem is based on the sense of separateness of the "ego" and every solution is based on the perception of reuniting with the Spirit. Ultimately, there is only one perceived problem and one solution.

ULTIMATELY THERE IS ONLY ONE PERCEIVED
PROBLEM AND ONE SOLUTION

6. **ILLUSION/TRUTH** Every perceived problem is based on the perceived separateness of your "ego" which in turn is based on your perception of yourself as a body, not as Spirit or Self. When you learn to identify with your higher Self rather than your body, you will begin to discover that the "ego" is an illusion. You will actually begin to remember that

the truth of who you are is your higher Self, your Spirit. You can choose to make the journey from the perceived illusory

THE "EGO" IS AN ILLUSION
THE TRUTH OF WHO YOU ARE
IS THE HIGHER SELF

experience of the separate "ego" to the truth of the united Self. For example, when you choose to forgive another person, you will no longer see them as a body separate from you. You will see them as a Spirit or Self joined with you. When you perceive someone as separate and different, you see them having good or bad qualities, traits or behaviors, and then judge them for it. Judgment in turn leads to grievances, anger, fear of attack and conflicted relationships. Forgiveness perceives the same Truth, Spirit and Self in another as in yourself. It thus leads to joining, healing, solutions and love.

7. **STRENGTHS/RESOURCES** As you begin to perceive yourself and others in terms of a united Self or Being, you begin to access a reservoir of strengths and resources within you which were previously unknown to you. You contact the Source within. Great strength, creativity, talent, power, freedom and resourcefulness exists within you. This Center

GREAT STRENGTH, CREATIVITY AND
RESOURCEFULNESS EXISTS WITHIN YOU

or Source is the Truth of who you are, your true Identity. When you rely on the illusory "ego", you will constantly experience yourself as weak, helpless, powerless, limited and bound. Call upon the unlimited strength, adaptability, imagination, joy and truth of your Spirit or Self. Close your eyes, relax and breathe deeply for 2 minutes. Next, imagine a switchboard in front of you with two switches; one labeled **E** for ego, one labeled **S** for Spirit or Self. The **E** switch is **on.**

Then, imagine yourself reaching out and turning the **E** switch to **off** and the **S** switch to **on**. Feel the strength, resourcefulness, creativity, power, love, peace and joy that dwells within you.

8. **OPEN-MINDEDNESS/FLEXIBILITY** You can discover that as you tap into the Truth of your Being, you become more and more open-minded and flexible. Consequently, you generate alternatives and possibilities to solving perceived problems more easily. You perceive problems in different ways and, in time, you will probably perceive less problems. What you previously saw as a problem, for example, when someone was angry with you, you will now perceive as a fearful person identified with their ego and calling for help or love from you. By being open-minded and flexible, you can offer love in a variety of ways and help the other person to return to the Truth of who they really are. You have joined with them by perceiving their true Self which is based on love, truth and oneness, instead of the ego based on anger, fear, illusion and separativeness. Consider where in your life you can benefit yourself and others by being more open-minded and flexible.

9. **WILLINGNESS/RECEPTIVITY** You can begin to make the journey from the problems created by the "ego" to the solutions of the Spirit or Self with a little willingness. This will help you forgive yourself and other people, see alternatives and possibilities, challenges and opportunities, gains and advantages where previously you saw only problems, difficulties, blocks, obstacles, failures and disappointments. Find yourself more receptive to new and creative ideas and to sources of unexpected inspiration. Find yourself reframing and re-perceiving situations, circumstances and relationships more easily and positively. All that you need is a little willingness and a receptive attitude. Then unseen forces will

enter your life, circumstances or relationships to help you. Close your eyes, relax and breathe slowly. Quiet your mind.

ALL YOU NEED IS A LITTLE WILLINGNESS
AND A RECEPTIVE ATTITUDE

Center yourself in your Being. Allow yourself to be receptive. Reflect briefly on some problem. Have a little willingness. Ask for an answer. Listen quietly for the answer.

10. **EVALUATE/ACT** With a little willingness and a receptive, quiet mind, you can ask within for an answer to a problem. Often you will receive an answer immediately. If you do not receive one the first time, then perhaps the second, third or fourth time you will. When you receive the answer, evaluate it and then act. By acting on the answer, you will commit

WHEN YOU RECEIVE THE ANSWER,
EVALUATE IT AND THEN ACT

yourself to solving the problem, reaching your goal, aligning yourself with your purpose and vision in life. It is important to evaluate the answer because the ego will frequently answer you first. If you experience any turmoil, conflict, uncertainty or internal debate, you are probably receiving an answer from your ego. If you feel totally certain, peaceful and confident, you are most likely receiving an answer from your higher Self or Being. Act, but be aware of the consequence of your action. If the consequence of your action brings you conflict and distress, reevaluate your decision and action and then listen within again. If the consequence of your action brings you peace, clarity and harmony, the answer was almost surely coming from your inner Self.

IF YOUR ACTION BRINGS CONFLICT,
LISTEN AGAIN

IF YOUR ACTION BRINGS PEACE,
IT WAS COMING FROM THE INNER SELF

11. **PRAYER/GUIDANCE** Prayer, along with meditation, is one of the most powerful ways to re-perceive problems, discover creative alternatives and possibilities, find solutions and heal relationships. When you pray, you ask that infinite/creative intelligence (divine/holy spirit) within your superconscious mind be your guide. This inner guidance puts you into contact with a powerful, inner force that has much more wisdom and love than your "ego" mind. Prayer allows you to access the deep truths within you, to discover hidden resources and strengths, to be open to divine inspiration, to heal old wounds, to love more profoundly, to find peace of mind, to

INNER GUIDANCE PUTS YOU IN CONTACT
WITH A POWERFUL, INNER FORCE;
PRAYER ALLOWS YOU TO ACCESS
THE DEEP TRUTHS WITHIN YOU

feel greater joy and to experience miraculous coincidences, events, healings or circumstances occurring in your life. It is through prayer that you can contact the universal or master mind or consciousness, sometimes referred to as Self, Being or God. Close your eyes now. Breathe slowly and deeply. Feel the love in your heart. Pray and ask for inner guidance.

12. **LET GO/RELEASE** After you have quieted your mind, prayed and asked for inner guidance from the infinite/creative intelligence or divine/holy spirit or energy, let go of your concerns, worries, wants and problems. By releasing them to a higher force, you are trusting in this inner power to guide and help you. The answer may come immediately or it may be delayed. Have faith that your prayers will be heard. Since the answer may not always come in the form you expect, it is always wise to ask that the solution you receive be for your

highest good and the highest good of everyone involved. While you are waiting to receive the answer, you can practice choosing peace, forgiving yourself and others, being grateful for the blessings you have already received and remembering that inherent within every disadvantage, loss, cost or problem is an equal or greater advantage, gain, benefit or solution.

LET GO AND RELEASE YOUR PROBLEMS
TO A HIGHER POWER

Reread the previous twelve steps. Deeply contemplate the significance of these ideas for your life. Do the suggested processes. Allow yourself to experience the inner transformation taking place.

Tim, single and in his late 20's, had a one year old child, Susan. His relationships with his attractive girlfriend Janet (24), the mother of this child, was quite ambivalent. Janet and Susan lived with Janet's manic-depressive father and placid mother. Tim was constantly judging himself for fathering Susan, not spending enough time with her, not really loving Janet, not having a better job (he worked in a grocery store) and for not furthering his education in the field of commercial art. He felt like a failure and constantly told himself, "I can't win". He resented Janet for the demands she placed on him and felt guilty that Susan lived in such a chaotic family environment. Despite this, he had a very good sense of humor, was a good musician and had a gentle disposition.

Tim's goals were to: like himself more; forgive himself, Janet and her family; return to school; have more fun; clarify and work out his relationship with Janet; change jobs or improve the quality of his job; spend more time with his daughter Susan; and to be happy again. A lot of therapy session time was spent on helping Tim reframe his way of seeing and thinking about things. His pessimistic attitude that, "I can't change the way I feel, think or act", was questioned until he gradually adopted the attitude, "I can feel, think and act differently", and then, "I will do it." His self-defeating attitude, "I shouldn't have gotten Janet pregnant and I should love Janet and want to be with her more" was gently challenged. I pointed out to Tim that the 11th commandment is "Thou Shalt Not Should On Oneself", and the 12th commandment is "Thou Shalt Not Should On Others". "Shoulding" on oneself produces guilt and anger at oneself, and "shoulding" on others generates anger and attack thoughts towards others.

As Tim was made aware of expectations and judgments that generated anger, hurt, guilt, depression, and a negative, self-defeating outlook on life, he was then able to let go of them. He learned to perceive that his love for Susan was genuine and that he cared for but did not love nor want to marry Janet. Janet soon realized she also did not love nor wish to marry Tim and needed to let go of her hurt and anger toward him.

When Tim started to think more positively, he started to feel better. He and Janet broke off their semi-dating relationship and started dating other people. Tim continued to love and support Susan, however. He went back to school, took graduate courses in art, and revitalized his desire to learn and grow. At the same time, he started a part-time evening job as a comedian and musician, which he really enjoyed. He also worked out some job conflicts using his new, more positive and hopeful outlook on life, and developed a new "win-win" attitude in relationships. When he discontinued his therapy sessions after ten months, he was a much happier, more self-confident person. Creative alternatives and possibilities had opened up in both Tim and Janet's lives.

When Gail first called me inquiring about the weekend seminar, I did not know that she had a serious physical illness (cancer) that might require surgery. Nor did I know that she had previously had radiation treatment for an earlier bout with cancer. She was clearly depressed, confused about the direction of her life, feeling hopeless, and having some serious relationship problems. She was in her early 50's, married and had three children. During the weekend seminar, it became apparent that she felt hatred for her elderly mother whom she felt rejected and neglected her. Not surprisingly, Gail avoided her mother as much as possible. She also had a very ambivalent, jealous relationship with her older, more successful sister. In addition, Gail was deeply concerned about her relationship with her children, some of whom were floundering around or had been involved with drugs. Though Gail was looking around for a job to give her some meaningful work and direction in her life, her husband had been quite successful in his career, though some impending financial problems worried her as well. He was generally supportive of her, however. Lonely, fearful and distraught, Gail eagerly attended the seminar.

Despite Gail's depressed mood, her obvious call for help (love) touched me early in the seminar. The seminar is designed to be a very safe, nurturing and loving environment for people to explore and heal themselves and their relationships. I facilitate it with the intention that everyone participates and that everyone, including the assistants and the facilitator, share love, compassion, forgiveness, healing and joy. The music, relaxation, meditation and guided imagery processes, for example, were created to open the heart. Gail apparently was particularly moved by these processes, especially the ones on forgiveness. She released intense hurt, pain, fear and anger at her mother and herself. She cried profusely. As she did, her heart opened and she experienced a tremendous love and compassion; first for her mother and then for herself. She "saw" for the first time all the suffering, abuse and neglect her elderly mother had experienced in her own life and felt deep empathy and sadness for her. Instead of contempt, she felt kindness. Instead of distance, she felt closeness. Instead of confusion, she felt understanding. Instead of darkness, she saw light. Gail's whole expression changed. A radiance and joyfulness emerged. She could hardly believe she felt so loving and compassionate toward her mother and could perceive her so differently. A deep peace settled over her.

In the ensuing months, many changes took place. She took her mother out for lunch immediately after the seminar, brought her flowers and genuinely enjoyed herself. Every week from then on, they had lunch together, and she soon started telling her mother she loved her. She started appreciating what she had received from her mother rather than focusing on what she had missed.

Gail also attended our advanced seminar on love, healing and well-being, and had an equally profound experience. She started to see me in weekly psychotherapy sessions for some months to consolidate and expand her gains. In these sessions, Gail focused especially on forgiving her sister, her children, and herself more, enhancing her self-esteem and exploring new, positive alternatives for her life. She did require surgery for her cancer and follow-up chemotherapy sessions, so she also had to deal with the physical and emotional effects of the treatment. I saw her in the hospital soon after the surgery. I was deeply moved by her courage as I was throughout the whole process of her growth and healing. She became increasingly more in touch with her higher Self/Being during this period of time through regular periods of meditation and visualization.

As her healing progressed (physical, emotional, relational, and spiritual), Gail started to think of starting her own business. A few months later she opened a specialty gift business and was very active, energetic, happy and enthusiastic. Her relationship with her sister and children was much improved and she continued to see and lovingly look after her mother. Clearly the love and caring in her heart had surfaced and was guiding her life to a much greater extent. A year and a half later, she discontinued the business and wrote a book. I felt most honored and privileged to have guided her through some part of the process and actually felt grateful to have learned, worked, and grown with her.

ALTERNATIVES POSSIBILITIES
HOME WORK/PLAY SHEET

UNDER "A", LIST TEN PERCEIVED PROBLEMS, OBSTACLES, DISAD-
VANTAGES, LOSSES, COSTS, FAILURES, GRIEVANCES, ILLNESSES,
CONFLICTS, OR DIFFICULTIES THAT YOU EXPERIENCE.

1. A.
   B.

2. A.
   B.

3. A.
   B.

4. A.
   B.

5. A.
   B.

6. A.
   B.

7. A.
   B.

8. A.
   B.

9. A.
   B.

10. A.
    B.

GO BACK OVER THE LIST AND UNDER "B", WRITE A POSSIBLE ALTER-
NATIVE, SOLUTION, CHALLENGE, OPPORTUNITY, ADVANTAGE, GAIN,
BENEFIT, FORGIVENESS, HEALING, LESSON, OR TEACHING FROM
EACH EXPERIENCE OR SITUATION. ASK THE CREATIVE/INFINITE IN-
TELLIGENCE THE DIVINE/HOLY SPIRIT, OR ENERGY WITHIN YOU FOR
GUIDANCE.

CHAPTER SIX

CREATING A SENSE OF ACCOMPLISHMENT AND SATISFACTION IN WORK, CAREER AND LIFE

You can create a deep sense of accomplishment and satisfaction in your work, career and life.

1. **ALTERNATIVES/POSSIBILITIES** Generate creative alternatives and possibilities for perceived problems in your life. Inherent within every perceived disadvantage, loss or cost is an equal or greater advantage, gain or benefit. Inherent within every problem is the solution. You can learn to welcome perceived problems as "good". Every perceived problem has at its root a sense of separateness. Every solution has at its root a sense of connectedness or unity. Separateness is perceived by the lower consciousness of your ego. It generates a sense of difference, specialness, judgment, fear and grievances. Connectedness or joining is perceived by the higher consciousness of your Self. It generates a sense of oneness, sameness, forgiveness, love and peace.

When problems are perceived through the lens of the ego, an illusion is seen instead of the truth. When you perceive

WHEN PROBLEMS ARE PERCEIVED
THROUGH THE LENS OF THE EGO,
AN ILLUSION IS SEEN
INSTEAD OF THE TRUTH

truth, you will contact strength and resourcefulness within and you will experience more open-mindedness and flexibility in problem solving. You will need a little willingness and receptivity. Then you can call upon prayer and inner guidance to help you.

2. **ACCOMPLISHMENT/SATISFACTION** You can develop a deep sense of accomplishment and satisfaction in your work and life. Begin to see problems and obstacles as stepping-stones, challenges and lessons. Then you will see that there are many gifts being sent to you by the universe in order to

ACCOMPLISHMENT AND SATISFACTION
ARE INNER EXPERIENCES
ALIGN YOUR CAREER GOALS
WITH YOUR PURPOSE AND
VISION IN LIFE

teach you something you need to learn. Accomplishment and satisfaction are inner experiences. Align your career goals with your purpose and vision in life. Then every task you complete becomes part of a sub-goal. These sub-goals in turn lead to your life goal which is in alignment with your vision and purpose in life. If your purpose and vision are aligned with the core of your Being, then every task completed, no matter how small, immediately becomes a source of inner accomplishment and satisfaction. Soon you will experience yourself moving progressively forward in alignment with your true Self, growing personally, professionally and spiritually.

3. **SUCCESS/FULFILLMENT** Success is often defined as the progressive achievement of worthy goals. Only you can define for yourself the worthy goals you choose for your own

SUCCESS IS THE PROGRESSIVE ACHIEVEMENT
OF WORTHY GOALS

purpose and vision in life. You can learn to define every activity you engage in and every experience you have as either successful or as a lesson, teaching or gift. Re-perceiving in this way leads you to experience a much greater sense of fulfillment in your work, career and life. Ultimately, a sense of success and fulfillment comes only from within, from the core

A SENSE OF SUCCESS AND FULFILLMENT
COMES ONLY FROM WITHIN

of your Being. It is not determined by other's perceptions, evaluations and judgments of you. For your own peace, you may, however, need to learn how to release self-judgments, criticisms, and negative self-evaluations arising from the "ego". Nothing you are doing or have ever done is sinful, bad or wrong, except through the illusory lens of the "ego". Past or present "mistakes" or errors are lessons and gifts, requiring correction and forgiveness. Appreciate yourself more and experience success and fulfillment. For one week, list five successes or fulfillments you experienced that day and five gifts/lessons you received or learned.

4. **HARMONY/BALANCE** Ultimately, a sense of success comes from a sense of fulfilling who you are, in alignment with your purpose and vision in life. You will, in turn, experience fulfillment in your work, career and life when you experience an inner harmony and balance. This can never be

attained by identification with the ego, ego goals, or external goals of the world; i.e., seeking for wealth, status, prestige, fame and physical objects. Ego goals arise from a sense of lack, incompletion, imbalance and disharmony. From this perspective, you will always be searching outside yourself for success and fulfillment. True harmony and balance come

TRUE HARMONY AND BALANCE COME FROM WITHIN

from within. When you are in alignment with the completeness and wholeness of your Being, your higher Self will express itself naturally. Close your eyes, breathe slowly and deeply. Relax. With a quiet mind, ask the infinite/creative intelligence within to help you experience a sense of harmony, balance and fulfillment.

5. **CAUSE/EFFECT** Every cause has an effect; every effect a cause. There are no accidents or coincidences (effects) without causes. If you identify the cause, you can change the effect. Thoughts or ideas are causes of effects (circumstances). Ideas or thoughts leave not their Source. Their Source

THOUGHTS OR IDEAS ARE CAUSES OF EFFECTS (CIRCUMSTANCES)

is either in the higher (super) consciousness of the Self or in the lower consciousness of the ego. Thoughts generated from the Self as Source bring inner harmony, balance, fulfillment, love, peace, joy and creative expression. Ideas generated from the "ego" as Source bring a sense of inner conflict, imbalance, fear, lack and blocks to creativity. Experiences are reflections of your thoughts and ideas and the Source from which they come. Contemplate your ideas and thoughts for a few minutes; and then their Source.

6. **CONTROL/FREEDOM** You can control the thoughts and ideas in your mind. Start now to access them from your superconscious mind rather than from your "ego" mind. Feelings and bodily sensations are effects. Thoughts are causes. You feel good (balanced) when you feel in control of yourself and feel bad (imbalanced) when you feel out of control. By identifying the cause (thoughts), you control the effects (feelings, bodily sensations). Then you will experience a

    BY IDENTIFYING THE CAUSE (THOUGHTS)
    YOU CONTROL THE EFFECTS (FEELINGS,
    BODILY SENSATIONS)

    greater sense of inner freedom. Inner freedom comes from being in control of your thoughts and ideas and, therefore, your feelings and sensations. In your work and life, you will experience a much greater sense of inner control and freedom when you learn, apply and master the law of cause and effect.

7. **EXPECTATION/ATTRACTION** Your expectations and beliefs arise from your thoughts and ideas. Your thoughts and ideas arise from your identification with your superconscious mind or your lower conscious mind (ego). Your identification with your superconscious mind allows you to experience the truth of your Identity/Self/Being which is strength and love. Your identification with your ego brings

    YOUR IDENTITY/SELF/BEING IS
    STRENGTH AND LOVE

    identification with illusion, fear and weakness. Your image of who you are, your Identity, determines your thoughts, ideas, expectations and beliefs. What you expect and believe, you attract. Like a magnet, you attract to you the people,

    WHAT YOU EXPECT AND BELIEVE, YOU ATTRACT

situations, circumstances and events in your life that harmonize with your Identity. Reflect for a few moments on your sense of Identity, your predominant thoughts, ideas, expectations and beliefs (causes) and who/what you attract to you (effects) in your work, career and life.

8. **CONCEPTION/ACHIEVEMENT** Your expectations and beliefs lead you to conceive and picture what you want to achieve; that is, your goals. What you believe and conceive (cause), you can achieve (effect). Conception is first an inner

WHAT YOU BELIEVE AND CONCEIVE (CAUSE), YOU CAN ACHIEVE (EFFECT)

experience (cause) and only later produces an outer event, the achievement (effect). The most satisfying and permanent achievements are in alignment with the higher purpose, vision and goals of your Self/Being. Achievements aligned with the goals of "ego", tend to give temporary, fleeting satisfaction and experiences of frustration and disappointment. You can believe, conceive and achieve what you choose. Close your eyes. Breathe slowly and deeply. Relax. Align your beliefs and expectations with your Self/Being. Then focus on what you believe, conceive and want to achieve.

9. **ADAPTATION/DEDICATION** In order to achieve your goals, you will need to have ideas, expectations, beliefs and conceptions (causes). Next, you will want to visualize your goals and consciously choose to create them. Then create and adapt, create and adjust, create and adapt, create and adjust, since movement toward your goal will be in a series of

CREATE AND ADAPT; CREATE AND ADJUST

steps or sub-goals. You might make mistakes or errors or be off target, but, nevertheless, by accepting the process, keeping your eye on your target (goal), creating, adjusting and staying in alignment with your true Self, you will achieve your goal. You will also need to be dedicated to your goals, purpose and vision in life. Dedication, along with persistence and determination, is a powerful quality for success, fulfillment and achievement. It is wise to constantly ask the infinite/creative intelligence within whether your goals are aligned with your highest purpose and vision, your true Self or Being. Try it now.

10. **COOPERATION/COMPASSION** You will achieve your goals more quickly and effectively by being willing to cooperate with others to help them achieve their own goals. This is a "win-win" attitude that requires willingness to listen and empathize with others wants and feelings. Since all minds are joined at the level of superconscious mind, your highest purpose, vision and goals for love, joy, fulfillment, harmony and balance are the same as the highest purpose and vision of other people. Consequently, you naturally experience compassion arising from your higher Self and desire to share it. Compassion joins and heals. Compassion both precedes and follows forgiveness. It leads easily to cooperation and joint attainment of goals for the highest good. Close

COMPASSION JOINS AND HEALS
COMPASSION PRECEDES AND FOLLOWS
FORGIVENESS

your eyes. Breathe slowly. Relax. Feel compassion in your heart. Picture yourself sharing compassion and cooperation with others in work and life.

11. **ENTHUSIASM/JOY** Enthusiasm, like compassion, comes from the higher Self, Being, or Spirit. Enthusiasm generates drive and success. The word actually means inspired and is derived from the word "theos", meaning God or spirit, and

"entos", meaning within. So enthusiasm literally means, "the spirit of God/Self/Being within you". Enthusiasm is infectious. When your work, career and life goals are aligned with

ENTHUSIASM MEANS "THE SPIRIT OF
GOD/SELF/BEING WITHIN YOU"

your purpose and vision, you will invariably experience great enthusiasm for whatever you are doing. When you tap into this God/Spirit within, you will experience joy. Joy comes from within. When you constantly experience joy, you will be a happy, fulfilled and contented person. You will bring this joy and enthusiasm to everything you do and experience. Even if you are not experiencing enthusiasm and joy this minute, act as if you feel them. Within a short time (sometimes immediately), you will begin to feel enthusiasm and joy.

12. SERVICE/CONTRIBUTION Experiences of enthusiasm, joy, compassion, cooperation, harmony, balance and fulfillment all arise from being in alignment with your highest purpose, vision and goals in life. These in turn arise from alignment with the core of your Being/Self/Spirit or superconscious mind. Increasingly this will lead to a natural desire to be of service to others. You will naturally find yourself

THIS WILL LEAD TO A NATURAL DESIRE
TO BE OF SERVICE
YOU WILL WANT TO CONTRIBUTE TO
THE WELL-BEING OF OTHERS

wanting to contribute to the well-being and welfare of others. Eventually, according to the law of karma or compensation ("as you give, so you receive; as you sow, so you reap"), you will experience joy returned with joy, love with love, and service with service. When, where and how this happens may surprise you. Yet, the more service and contribution you offer, coming from the love, compassion and harmony of your heart, the more joy, accomplishment, satisfaction and fulfillment you'll experience in your work, career and life. Close your eyes. Breathe deeply. Relax. Contact the joy and compassion in your heart. Visualize yourself offering loving service and contribution to others.

Reread the twelve guidelines for creating a sense of accomplishment and satisfaction in your work and life. Practice the processes and exercises. Lesson by lesson, day by day, gradually and sometimes dramatically, you will improve the quality and well-being of your work, career and life.

John, 25, single and living at home with his parents, was confused, anxious and had difficulty concentrating. He was a delivery man for a small drug store and his long-range goal was to be financially independent. His short range goal was to own some real estate. I taught him relaxation, visualization, the creation and manifestation process, plus positive self-talk. He constantly pictured his goal of owning real estate property, developing the ability to concentrate and increasing his self-confidence. Every day he listened to self-improvement tapes that helped him to relax, concentrate, enhance his self-esteem, visualize what he wanted, choose to create his goals and to act on his intentions and decisions.

After seeing me for two and one-half months, John became very eager to attend an intensive, seven-day real estate course costing $1500 that was being conducted in Georgia. I was a bit skeptical of its value, but by this time, John's concentration and confidence had improved substantially so he wrote for brochures on the course and made several phone calls acquiring information. Then he sent in his deposit check for $500.00. John was eager to attend. One week later he was shocked to receive a phone call telling him that his deposit had arrived too late and the class of 20 was filled. He was extremely disappointed and frustrated. Despite this unfortunate appearing experience, John persisted in his determination to learn the skills needed for owning real estate.

I saw John for five months on a weekly basis. When we ended our therapy sessions, John felt relaxed, self-confident and able to concentrate. He had finally been able to read real estate magazines, manuals and books, and had attended local real estate seminars. Three months later, I called him. For very little money down, John had just purchased a small apartment building in Philadelphia worth $80,000. He was excited and delighted that he had attained his first major goal and felt on his way to financial independence.

ACCOMPLISHMENT/SATISFACTION HOME WORK/PLAY SHEET

A. WRITE DOWN A SERIES OF THREE SUB-GOALS LEADING TO A LARGER GOAL THAT LEADS TO YOUR PURPOSE AND VISION IN LIFE.
    1. SUB-GOAL 1:
    2. SUB-GOAL 2:
    3. SUB-GOAL 3:
    4. GOAL:
    5. PURPOSE AND VISION:

B. WRITE DOWN FIVE SUCCESSES/FULFILLMENTS (ACCOMPLISH-MENTS/SATISFACTIONS) YOU'VE HAD:

TODAY:

1.
2.
3.
4.
5.

THIS WEEK:

1.
2.
3.
4.
5.

THIS MONTH:

1.
2.
3.
4.
5.

THIS YEAR:

1.
2.
3.
4.
5.

DURING THE LAST FIVE YEARS:

1.
2.
3.
4.
5.

DURING YOUR LIFE:

1.
2.
3.
4.
5.

C.   WRITE DOWN FIVE EXPECTATIONS, BELIEFS, CONCEPTIONS YOU HOLD:

    1.

    2.

    3.

    4.

    5.

D.   WRITE DOWN FIVE EFFECTS AND FIVE CAUSES IN YOUR LIFE:

EFFECT:	CAUSE:
1.	1.
2.	2.
3.	3.
4.	4.
5.	5.

E.   LIST FIVE WAYS YOU'VE SERVED OR CONTRIBUTED TO OTHERS

THIS MONTH:
    1.
    2.
    3.
    4.
    5
THIS YEAR:
    1.
    2.
    3.
    4.
    5.

REPEAT THIS EXERCISE AT LEAST ONCE PER MONTH.

CHAPTER SEVEN

CREATING AND DEVELOPING HIGH SELF-ESTEEM AND SELF-LOVE

There are twelve guidelines for creating and developing a sense of high self-esteem and self-love.

1. **ACCOMPLISHMENT/SATISFACTION** The inner experience of accomplishment and satisfaction comes from establishing a set of worthy goals in alignment with your purpose and vision in life. Success is the progressive achievement of worthy goals. Fulfillment comes when you do what you love to do; when you express your talents and abilities from the creative core of your Being. Ultimately, a lasting

    FULFILLMENT COMES WHEN YOU DO
    WHAT YOU LOVE TO DO;
    WHEN YOU EXPRESS YOURSELF
    FROM THE CREATIVE CORE OF YOUR BEING

    sense of success and fulfillment can only occur when you experience an inner harmony and balance. It can never occur when you are identified with external "ego" goals arising from a sense of lack, like the "need" for status, money and possessions. Every cause has an effect. Thoughts and ideas are causes. When they arise from Self/Being as Source, they will bring you harmony, balance, peace, fulfillment. When they arise from the ego as source, they will bring you conflict, fear, disharmony and imbalance. You can learn to control your thoughts and ideas (causes) and, therefore, your feelings, bodily sensations and achievements (effects). Your expectations, beliefs and conceptions arise from your thoughts and ideas. What you expect, believe and conceive (causes), you attract and achieve (effects). Your ideas, thoughts, expectations, beliefs and conceptions are based on your perception of yourself. This self-image, in turn, is based on your identification with either the superconscious mind, (your true Self/Being) or with the illusion of your "ego" mind.

2. SELF-ESTEEM/SELF-LOVE You can develop high self-esteem by learning to value yourself. There is no one on the planet just like you. No one has the same combination of interests, abilities, resources, physique, style or personality. So

THERE IS NO ONE ON THE PLANET JUST LIKE YOU

learn to appreciate yourself more. List ten qualities that you hold in high esteem about yourself. If necessary, ask other people to assist you. Don't be shy or embarrassed. Imagine that your best friend is helping you write this list. Be aware of any emotions or judgments that arise. Close your eyes, relax and picture a blackboard. Visualize your friend walking up to the blackboard and listing these ten positive qualities about you. Picture an audience of people watching this and applauding. Learning to love yourself more is a prerequisite to loving others. Write a love letter thanking yourself for every kind, loving or talented thing you ever did for yourself or another. Acknowledge yourself. Appreciate yourself. Love yourself. Allow yourself to be loved. Close

ACKNOWLEDGE YOURSELF; APPRECIATE YOURSELF; LOVE YOURSELF

your eyes. Breathe deeply. Relax. Picture yourself esteeming, loving and feeling good about yourself. Make a commitment to do three loving, nurturing things for yourself this week and every week for ten weeks.

3. SELF-TALK/SELF-WORTH Your ability to esteem and love yourself will depend on self-talk. Positive, loving self-talk arising from the core of your Being will lift and support you. Negative, attacking self-talk arising from your "ego" will depress and discourage you. Consciously learn to engage in more positive, loving self-talk and, in the process, enhance your self-worth. One way you can do this is by identifying and letting go of judgments, criticisms and attacks on yourself. Stop "shoulding" on yourself: "I should have done, thought, felt a certain way." List all your negative judgments, beliefs and attitudes toward yourself in one column. Close your eyes. Relax. Ask that the creative/infinite intelligence (divine/holy spirit or energy) help you to substitute positive beliefs, attitudes and thoughts for negative ones. Then, in a second column, list the alternative, positive beliefs, attitudes and thoughts. The negative self-talk of your "ego" functions as an inner enemy, slowly destroying you by generating fear, hurt, disappointment, rejection, anger and sickness and ruining your relationships. Positive affirmations, such as "I like myself", or "I love myself", repeated while looking in a mirror, walking, driving, or listening to music serve as excellent positive self-talk. Other positive affirmations include, "I am valuable", "I am lovable", "I am competent", "God/Self/Being loves me", "I am worthwhile", "I am loved", "I am strong and

I AM VALUABLE; I AM LOVABLE; I AM WORTHWHILE; I AM LOVED

powerful and healthy". Make up your own. Repeat them 50 to 100 times per day.

4.   RIGHT/HAPPY You have a choice in life between being right or being happy. Many people prefer to be right and makes others wrong. In the process, they engage in a great

YOU HAVE A CHOICE IN LIFE BETWEEN
BEING RIGHT AND BEING HAPPY

deal of negative other-talk which generates grievances, anger, attacks and criticisms toward others; it also generates unhappiness. It reflects a judgmental mind, arising from the "ego". This same judgmental mind will later turn around and make you wrong and someone else or some other way right. You will constantly be unhappy and your self-esteem, love and self-worth will be diminished. You can learn to choose to be happy rather than being right (or wrong). Stop sorting, categorizing and judging yourself and others. Learn to forgive. You can choose peace, love, acceptance and happiness for yourself in all situations and circumstances. Ask the creative/infinite intelligence within you to help. In doing so, you will reconnect with your superconscious mind, your Self/Being, and see yourself as love. Close your eyes. Breathe deeply. Relax. Center yourself. Ask within to let go of your tendency to sort, categorize and judge yourself and others; to let go of grievances, hurts and resentments; to forgive yourself and others. Quiet your mind. Breathe deeply again. Be at peace.

5.   SELF-RESPECT/SELF-CONFIDENCE You can learn to respect yourself. First, however, you must learn to accept yourself. When you let go of judgmental attitudes, you learn to just accept yourself as you are. Do this by learning how to stop comparing yourself with other people. Stop comparing yourself with how you used to be or would like to be. Say, "I

am me", "I accept me as I am", "I respect and appreciate myself as I am". When you respect yourself more, you will respect and appreciate others more; you will develop more self-confidence. To help yourself develop more confidence, tell yourself, "I can do it"; then, "I will do it". Plan a series of

TELL YOURSELF: "I CAN DO IT – I WILL DO IT"

small, progressive changes in your life. Visualize them happening. For example, gradually be more appropriately assertive, express your feelings, compliment someone, speak highly of yourself, develop a new ability, invite someone to lunch, make that telephone call, express gratitude to another. Decide on two new actions for this week to enhance your self-respect and confidence.

6.   JOURNEY/AWAKEN You are on a journey through life. From the moment of birth, you have been exposed to an infinite number of situations to learn from while on this journey. You have developed many skills, abilities, capacities and coping resources. You have had many opportunities to discover who you truly are, to awaken from the dream that guided you on your journey. Your dream was usually guided by your "ego" and so you sought after "ego" goals. Not knowing who you were, you usually sought for happiness, peace, joy, fulfillment outside yourself. You can awaken now to your true Self, to the core of your Being. Your journey through the illusory path of the "ego" can never bring you real

YOU CAN AWAKEN TO YOUR TRUE SELF,
TO THE CORE OF YOUR BEING

contentment, satisfaction, deep self-worth, self-esteem, self-respect or self-love. Contact the truth of who you are by being willing to release your attachment to your "ego". You can ask for help from the creative/infinite intelligence within you. Try it now.

7. RECOGNIZE/REMEMBER You will awaken from the dream on the journey through life when you recognize your true Self. You have forgotten who you are and identified with

AWAKEN FROM THE DREAM

idols and images that block your perception of the truth. You are not your body, appearance, sexuality, weight, role, function, interests, talents, career, profession, or even your personality. Recognize the truth of who you are. Learn to remember who you are. Memory is a skill. You can learn to

RECOGNIZE THE TRUTH OF WHO YOU ARE

direct your memory from both painful and pleasant experiences in the past towards remembering your true Self, the core of your Being, in the present. Usually the process is gradual, sometimes sudden. Close your eyes. Breathe slowly and deeply. Contemplate the question, "Who am I?", over and over: "Who am I, really?". Ask the creative/infinite intelligence, the divine/holy spirit within to help you. Meditate, contemplate or pray for inner guidance.

8. IDENTITY/ESSENCE Your true Identity is not your "ego" but your Self/Being. It is not your body, but your Spirit, your Essence the core of who you are: love, peace, joy, happiness, creativity and abundance. It is aligned with your superconscious mind. Your Essence can never be changed. It is permanent, eternal and constant. It contains everything you need. It both precedes and transcends your interests, abilities, skills, roles, function and personality. When you recognize and remember your true Identity, you will immediately love yourself because you will perceive that you

YOUR TRUE IDENTITY, YOUR ESSENCE
IS LIGHT AND LOVE

are light and love. You will immediately respect and appreciate yourself because you are worthiness. You will perceive yourself as innocent or holy, not guilty, sinful or bad as your "ego" perceives you. See that your Essence is always at peace. Only "ego" creates turmoil or conflict. Perceive your "ego" as false, an illusion, a mis-perception of who you truly are. You will see that you are infinitely more valuable than you thought you were. Learn to perceive the truth of your Identity/Essence.

9. PERFECTION/WHOLENESS The essence of your Self/Being, your true Identity, is always perfect, complete and whole. Your "ego", however, experiences itself as imperfect,

THE ESSENCE OF YOUR SELF/BEING IS PERFECT, COMPLETE AND WHOLE

incomplete and lacking. This generates fear, guilt, anger, frustration and disappointment, while it looks outside itself for wholeness, completeness and perfection. The key to experiencing your self as whole, complete and perfect lies within, not without. As you learn to connect with that place of inner perfection and wholeness, you will experience self-esteem, love and worth. You will find yourself perceiving the perfection, wholeness and completeness of others. Discover that what you see in others, you see in yourself; and what you see in yourself, you will see in others. Since what you focus on expands, as you focus on the perfection, wholeness and completeness of others, it will expand. Every day this week (and then this month), begin to focus on the perfection, wholeness and completeness of yourself and others.

10. LIGHT/BEAUTY Your Identity and Essence is light. This light of the inner Self/Being is radiant, loving, gentle and peaceful. It is perfect, whole and complete. Identify with the light of your Being, rather than the darkness of your "ego"

which generates fear and mistrust. As you learn to contact the inner light, begin to see the inner beauty. This inner light and inner beauty will become more and more apparent to you. Practicing forgiveness will help you let go of resentments, grievances, hurtful, painful and guilty feelings, the darkness of the "ego". As you practice forgiveness, you will discover your true Identity: light and beauty. Contemplation,

> *PRACTICING FORGIVENESS WILL HELP YOU*
> *DISCOVER YOUR INNER BEAUTY*

meditation, visualization and/or prayer can help you. So can reading or listening to inspired, uplifting material or music. Once again, close your eyes. Relax. Breathe deeply. Perhaps listen to some soothing music. Go deeply within. Ask that the infinite/creative intelligence within guide you to a deeper experience of your inner light, your inner beauty. Be patient. Try this exercise several times.

11. UNIQUENESS/SAMENESS You are a unique, wonderful manifestation of the inner light. The Self/Being, which is your true Identity, expresses itself through you in a unique way. No two people have the same personality, interests, physique, style, manner or role that you do. You are like a flower or snowflake; one of a kind. You are a precious, beautiful jewel. Learn to love the beautiful uniqueness which expresses itself in your form. Even so, the Essence/Identity of who you are, the Light, Self, Being and Spirit is the same within everyone. Your manifestation is unique and yet your Essence, the Core of your Identity is the same. You might compare it to light going through a prism

> *YOUR MANIFESTATION IS UNIQUE*
> *AND YET YOUR ESSENCE,*
> *THE CORE OF YOUR BEING,*
> *IS THE SAME*

which becomes a spectrum of colors. Yet, the unique colors arise from the same light. Reflect on your uniqueness; then your sameness. Contemplate others uniqueness and sameness.

12. GREATNESS/MAGNIFICENCE Your Essence is not only complete, whole and perfect, not only filled with light and beauty, not only filled with love and peace, it is also great and magnificent. Experience your greatness and magnificence.

YOUR ESSENCE IS GREAT AND MAGNIFICENT

As you perceive these things, you will perceive the greatness and magnificence in others. Your mind is like a mirror. What you see in others, you see in yourself. Your mind is like a magnet. If you experience greatness and magnificence within, you draw people to you who you will perceive as great and magnificent. The more you forgive others, the more you will perceive their greatness and magnificence; their true Identity. The more you forgive yourself, the more you will see, remember and recognize your greatness and magnificence. The more you forgive, the more you will be free of the smallness, insignificance and limits of the bound "ego". The more you forgive, the more you will contact the greatness, magnificence and freedom of your Self. Let your inner guide help you. Close your eyes. Breathe deeply. Relax. Go deep within. Ask the creative/infinite intelligence (divine/holy spirit or energy) within to guide you to your true Identity, your Essence, beyond the fearful "ego" to the light, love, greatness and magnificence of your true Being.

Reread these twelve guidelines frequently, preferably once per day. Practice the exercises. Be patient and yet persistent. Gradually and sometimes suddenly, you will discover and experience your true Identity, self-esteem and self-worth; love, light, greatness and magnificence

Joe came to see me after being in an accident. He was emotionally distressed and his upper back, neck and shoulder were still causing him great pain. At 41, he was unhappy with his life. Joe was separated from his wife and working in a family business. He disliked his father who co-ran the business with his mother. Joe was angrily jealous of his 32 year old, flamboyant younger sister who had a much more responsible position than he did. He tolerated his two younger brothers who also worked in the business. Joe's family accused him of being tense, irritable, on edge, and ready to explode. Generally, the rest of his family, except his mother, kept their distance from him. His father would rarely talk to him. Not surprisingly, Joe was very self-critical, as well as critical of his family. His self-esteem was low. Although he was bright, talented and articulate, he depended on his family for his economic livelihood. Moreover, though separated from his wife of many years, he lived in the same house with her. In this way, they shared the parenting and finances of raising their teenage daughter.

In the early sessions, Joe seemed to benefit the most from relaxation and visualization exercises. His emotional and physical stress level began to decrease and he had less physical pain. His family saw that he was less on edge, more relaxed, and easier to get along with. Family sessions with his mother, brothers and sister, and "couple" sessions with both parents helped to improve communication in the family. These sessions also revealed that the other family members were even more distressed by his younger sister, who was a drug abuser. Joe practiced his affirmations to enhance self-esteem and self-worth, along with self-forgiveness and self-awareness exercises to reduce negative self-talk and self-depreciation. I constantly encouraged him to love and respect himself more so he could learn to give love and respect to others. I encouraged him to explore other career alternatives, since he was only using some of his many skills. Eventually, Joe found part-time work in the electronic media field and started working toward developing his own business. With higher self-esteem, he was calmer and relaxed and his relationships with his family improved substantially. He and his wife moved to another home which removed some tensions in that relationship.

An unusual event occurred during the course of our sessions. One morning I received a phone call from a very nasty and angry lawyer. I did not know the lawyer and was startled to hear him abrasively order me to immediately terminate therapy with Joe and send him a final report. Initially I was shaken by the force of the lawyer's voice and the obvious attack. Later I discovered that the lawyer represented Joe in his accident insurance claim. The lawyer wanted to file suit against the other party for damages and injury and believed he couldn't proceed until the therapy sessions were discontinued. Even amidst the distress I felt from the suddenness of the demanding and abrasive call, I knew the lawyer was at some level calling for help and love. After he hung up, I knew that I had to quiet and center myself and generate some creative alternatives to this highly unexpected problem. I took ten minutes to relax, meditate and send peace and love to this lawyer. I also discussed the situation with a close friend.

Then, coming from a more centered and calm space, I made a series of phone calls to Joe, the insurance company, and the referring physician. I discovered that the lawyer had made an equally abrasive call to the referring physician's office and an only slightly less attacking call to Joe. I did not know what the lawyer was fearful of but I knew he was afraid of something. Several times over the next few days, I meditated and visualized sending the lawyer peace and love and asked the creative/infinite intelligence (divine/holy spirit) to resolve this matter harmoniously and for the highest good. I also practiced forgiving him for attacking me. Eventually I discovered that the lawyer was also being pressured to use his influence to terminate the case so that Joe's insurance company wouldn't have to pay any further disability claims. When I next spoke to the lawyer, I was better prepared and much more centered. When he began to talk abrasively to me, I interrupted him and told him firmly that I would only converse with him if he talked to me respectfully in a manner in which professionals were accustomed to conducting business. He calmed down somewhat and we agreed to an exchange of written information. During the next two weeks, I often meditated and mentally surrounded the lawyer with light.

When I next spoke to the lawyer, the matter had been resolved. He apologized to me profusely, telling me how he had been overworked and overwhelmed by backlogged cases. He sounded much more relaxed. He thanked me for the report I had sent him on Joe's condition and progress to date (with Joe's permission, of course), thanked me for my handling of the matter and apologized again. He was very sweet this time. I did continue to see Joe in therapy for a few more months.

I relearned some important lessons from this experience.

1.   Prepare for unexpected stressors occurring in life.

2.   Attack, abuse or demands of any kind cover up hurt or fear and are always disguised calls for help and love.

3.   The stress that the attacking party is under is often part of a complicated network of relationships or institutions.

4.   Whenever there is anger or fear being displayed, the "ego" is always involved.

5.   Whatever the problem, love, peace and forgiveness are always cornerstones of the solution.

6.   When I am centered, coming from a place of calm and ask for guidance from the creative/infinite intelligence within me, I arrive at much more creative, harmonious and peaceful solutions to problems.

SELF-ESTEEM/SELF-LOVE HOME WORK/PLAY SHEET: A FOUR MONTH PROGRAM

FIRST MONTH:

A.   LIST TEN POSITIVE QUALITIES THAT YOU VALUE IN YOURSELF:

    1.

    2.

    3.

    4.

    5.

    6.

    7.

    8.

    9.

    10.

B.   VISUALIZE A FRIEND WALKING UP TO A BLACKBOARD AND LIST-ING FIVE ADDITIONAL POSITIVE QUALITIES ABOUT YOU. WRITE THEM DOWN:

    1.

    2.

    3.

    4.

    5.

C.   VISUALIZE AN AUDIENCE WATCHING YOUR FRIEND WRITE THESE POSITIVE QUALITIES ON THE BLACKBOARD AND APPLAUDING.

D.   WRITE A LETTER TO YOURSELF ACKNOWLEDGING AND THANK-ING YOURSELF FOR EVERY POSITIVE, LOVING THING YOU'VE DONE IN THE LAST FIVE YEARS.

E.   LIST FIVE LOVING, NURTURING THINGS THAT YOU ARE WILLING TO DO FOR YOURSELF THIS WEEK AND EVERY WEEK FOR FOUR WEEKS:

    1.

    2.

    3.

    4.

    5.

F.   IN COLUMN A, LIST FIVE NEGATIVE THOUGHTS, ATTITUDES, BELIEFS, JUDGMENTS, SHOULDS AND SELF-TALK YOU MAKE ABOUT YOURSELF. IN COLUMN B, LIST FIVE POSITIVE THOUGHTS, ATTITUDES, BELIEFS AND SELF-TALK YOU ARE WILL-ING TO SUBSTITUTE FOR THE NEGATIVE ONES IN COLUMN A. (CLOSE YOUR EYES AND ASK THE CREATIVE/INFINITE INTEL-LIGENCE WITHIN YOU TO HELP.)

COLUMN A   COLUMN B

    1.   1.

    2.   2.

    3.   3.

    4.   4.

    5.   5.

G.   LIST THREE POSITIVE AFFIRMATIONS THAT YOU ARE WILLING TO SAY (AFFIRM) TO YOURSELF REPEATEDLY TO ENHANCE YOUR SELF-ESTEEM (i LOVE MYSELF, i LIKE MYSELF, i AM VALUABLE, STRONG, CONFIDENT, COMPETENT, HEALTHY, CAPABLE OR WORTHY. GOD/SELF/BEING LOVES ME, ETC.).

    1.

    2.

    3.

REPEAT THE AFFIRMATIONS WHILE LOOKING IN THE MIRROR FOR FIVE MINUTES PER DAY. ALSO REPEAT THEM TO YOURSELF 50-100 TIMES THROUGHOUT THE DAY.

SECOND MONTH:

H. REPEAT TO YOURSELF, "I CAN DO IT", OR "I WILL DO IT", OVER AND OVER. LIST EIGHT ACTIONS YOU CAN AND WILL TAKE TO IN-CREASE YOUR SELF-CONFIDENCE (TWO OF WHICH YOU WILL DO THIS WEEK). THEN VISUALIZE THEM HAPPENING. THEN DO TWO MORE ACTIONS PER WEEK FOR THE NEXT THREE WEEKS.

1.   5.

2.   6.

3.   7.

4.   8.

ASK THE CREATIVE/INFINITE INTELLIGENCE (DIVINE/HOLY SPIRIT OR ENERGY) WITHIN TO HELP YOU.

I. CONTEMPLATE THE QUESTION "WHO AM I?", "WHO AM I REALLY?" ASK THE CREATIVE/INFINITE INTELLIGENCE, DIVINE/HOLY SPIRIT WITHIN TO HELP YOU. DO THIS FOR FIVE MINUTES PER DAY WITH YOUR EYES CLOSED FOLLOWING A BRIEF RELAXATION PROCESS. PRAY FOR INNER GUIDANCE.

J. FOR ONE WEEK, FOCUS ON THE PERFECTION, WHOLENESS AND COMPLETENESS OF EVERYONE AND EVERYTHING INCLUDING YOURSELF. NOTICE THAT WHAT YOU FOCUS ON EXPANDS.

K. FOR A SECOND WEEK, FOCUS ONLY ON THE INNER LIGHT, THE INNER BEAUTY OF YOURSELF AND OTHER PEOPLE. NOTICE THAT WHAT YOU FOCUS ON EXPANDS. ASK THE CREATIVE/INFINITE IN-TELLIGENCE, THE DIVINE/HOLY SPIRIT OR ENERGY TO HELP YOU.

L. FOR A THIRD WEEK, CONTEMPLATE FIRST THE POSITIVE, UNIQUE QUALITIES OF EVERY PERSON YOU MEET AS WELL AS YOURSELF, AND THEN CONTEMPLATE HOW YOU AND EVERY PERSON YOU MEET ARE THE SAME.

M. FOR THE FOURTH WEEK, CONTEMPLATE THE GREATNESS AND MAGNIFICENCE OF EVERY PERSON YOU MEET. ALSO CON-TEMPLATE YOUR OWN GREATNESS AND MAGNIFICENCE.

NOTICE HOW YOUR MIND IS LIKE A MIRROR AND HOW YOUR MIND IS LIKE A MAGNET.

THIRD MONTH:

N.   PRACTICE FORGIVING YOURSELF AND EVERYONE YOU HAVE EVER HELD A JUDGMENT, GRIEVANCE OR RESENTMENT TOWARD. PRACTICE THIS EVERY DAY FOR ONE MONTH.

FOURTH MONTH:

O.   PRACTICE LOVING YOURSELF AND EVERYONE ELSE UNCONDITIONALLY FOR ONE MONTH. OBSERVE YOUR PERCEPTIONS AND EMOTIONAL REACTIONS.   ASK THE CREATIVE/INFINITE INTELLIGENCE TO HELP YOU.

NOTES:

CHAPTER EIGHT

CREATING AND DEVELOPING INNER PEACE AND INNER SECURITY IN LIFE

It is important to create and develop inner peace and inner security in life. The following twelve steps will help you.

1   **SELF-ESTEEM/SELF-LOVE** You are a unique person with talents, abilities, resources, roles, functions, and a personality that exists nowhere else. You can learn to esteem,

> *YOU ARE A UNIQUE PERSON*
> *YOU CAN LEARN TO ESTEEM, RESPECT*
> *AND LOVE YOURSELF*

respect and love your uniqueness; to let go of negative self-talk and judgments about yourself; and to replace negative self-talk with positive self-talk and affirmations. Learn to choose to be happy rather than right. Learn to forgive yourself and others. At the same time in your journey through life, awaken from the false dream you live, release your identification with your "ego", and learn to recognize and remember that your true Self/Being is who you really are. Your true Identity, the core of who you are, is not your false "ego", but your Essence/Self/Being which is always perfect, whole and complete. It consists of love, light, beauty and abundance, and is characterized by greatness and magnificence. It is the same within everyone, yet you are a unique manifestation of this inner Light/Essence/Self.

2. **PEACE/SECURITY** Peace and security dwell within you at the core of your Being/Self. You will never find inner peace

PEACE AND SECURITY DWELL WITHIN YOU
AT THE CORE OF YOUR BEING/SELF

by searching outside in relationships, achievements, possessions, prestige, money, and accomplishments. The "ego" experiences itself as lacking and incomplete so it searches for external objects or people in order to find peace. You can find peace and security by turning within to your Self/Being, by reconnecting with your Identity/Essence. Close your eyes. Relax. Take slow, deep, breaths. Repeat the words "calm" and "relax" on the in and out breaths. Then repeat "peace" and "love" a few times. Between the in and out breaths, hold your breath for a count of three. Next visualize yourself in an elevator slowly descending from the tenth floor to the first floor. As the elevator descends, allow yourself to go deeper and deeper to the center of your Being/Self. Allow yourself to become calmer and calmer, more and more relaxed, more and more at peace, more and more secure. Then ask the creative/infinite intelligence within you (the divine/holy spirit or energy) to help you feel the deep sense of inner peace and security.

3. **QUIET/SAFETY** You can learn to quiet your mind, which is usually controlled by your "ego", busy sorting, comparing, judging, criticizing, making right and wrong. It agitates your mind and upsets your emotions. Learn to still the thought waves of your mind. When you do this, you will experience

LEARN TO STILL THE THOUGHT WAVES
OF YOUR MIND

an inner quietness, serenity, peace, and a sense of inner safety. You will be contacting the Self/Being within, your true Identity/Essence. Repeat the exercise described in Step 2. This time, however, when you get to the first floor, visualize the doors of the elevator opening. Picture yourself walking out to a quiet, peaceful, secure, loving and beautiful environment. It is important that you choose an environment (inner sanctuary) that is safe, secure, peaceful, quiet and relaxing. Allow yourself to look, feel, taste and touch it, and simultaneously experience the quietness, security, safety and peace deep within you.

4. **STRENGTH/FREEDOM** When your mind is quiet and at peace, when you feel safe and secure, you will discover a dynamic inner strength. You can access this inner strength and, at the same time, learn to feel powerful, capable and competent. Let go of perceiving yourself as vulnerable, helpless and a victim. These are all characteristics of the "ego". Learn to release yourself from inner restrictions that your "ego" uses to imprison and limit you and learn to develop inner freedom. Inner freedom and inner strength can be found by stilling your "ego" mind. Then you can ask creative/infinite intelligence to help you see alternatives and possibilities you didn't see before. Let go of grievances, resent-

INNER FREEDOM AND STRENGTH CAN BE FOUND
BY STILLING THE "EGO" MIND

ments and hurts that create blocks, barriers and obstacles to experiencing your power, strength and freedom. Forgive yourself and others and make choices and decisions to manifest your goals. Learn to experience gratitude and blessings.

5. **GENTLENESS/INNOCENCE** You will discover the gentleness within you when you have learned to quiet your mind and have begun to experience inner peace and safety. When you are gentle and compassionate with yourself and gentle and compassionate with others, your "ego" mind will quiet down. You will experience more peace, security and safety. As you learn to be more gentle, less judgmental and critical of yourself, you will find it easier to discover that you are not and have never been bad, wrong, stupid, sinful, guilty or evil. Your true Identity/Essence was, is, and always will be innocent. Gentleness helps you experience your innocence,

    YOUR TRUE IDENTITY/ESSENCE WAS, IS,
    AND ALWAYS WILL BE INNOCENT

    beauty, light, love and magnificence, all the qualities of your Self/Being. Close your eyes. Perhaps put on some soothing music. Breathe slowly and deeply. Repeat "calm and relaxed", "peace and love". Visualize the journey down the elevator to the inner sanctuary. When you are in there, allow yourself to feel your gentleness, strength, innocence and love. Allow yourself to feel cleansed and free of all limitations. Then visualize yourself offering gentleness, innocence, love, light and strength to someone else.

6. **HEART/MIND** When you learn to quiet the agitated thought waves of your "ego" mind, you will begin to open your heart and access your "superconscious" mind. Your superconscious mind, your heart center and your Self/Being are all interconnected. As you open your heart, experience more love for yourself and others. Forgive yourself and others. Be

    AS YOU OPEN YOUR HEART, EXPERIENCE MORE LOVE
    FOR YOURSELF AND OTHERS

gentler and kinder, be more understanding and empathic and you will discover the profound light and warmth in the center of your heart. Your Essence consists of love, light and warmth. When you are in your "inner sanctuary", open your heart to the depths of your love; access your superconscious mind, align yourself with your Self/Being, your Identity/Essence. You can ask the creative/infinite intelligence (the divine/holy spirit) to help you experience the love and light within you. Try it now.

7. **ACCEPTANCE/APPRECIATION** Your true Identity/Essence is love, light, strength and magnificence. When you learn to accept yourself as you are and to accept your true Identity, you will markedly enhance your inner security and peace. This means you need to stop "shoulding" on yourself (I should have done, thought, felt this or that), to stop judging yourself, and to accept yourself as you are. Appreciate the inner light that shines forth in the expression of your Being. Learn to do this now. As you learn to appreciate yourself, you will be aligned with your true integrity. You will become true to your Self. Begin to experience greater inner

APPRECIATE THE INNER LIGHT THAT
SHINES FORTH IN YOUR BEING

strength free from limitations and restrictions. Acceptance and appreciation of yourself will quiet your mind and greatly enhance your inner peace. Reflect for a few minutes on how you can accept and appreciate yourself more. Look in the mirror with love, acceptance, appreciation and gratitude for several minutes. Allow yourself to feel inner peace and security as you do so.

8. **VALIDATE/HONOR** By learning how to accept and appreciate yourself, you are also learning how to validate yourself. You are communicating value to yourself by giving

yourself a stamp of approval, by telling yourself you are okay as you are, with all your feelings, likes, dislikes, interests, peculiarities, and habits. Then you will be ready to take the next step, which is honoring yourself. To honor yourself is to consider yourself worthy of profound respect and importance just because you are you; just because you have been created by the Creator. When you learn how to accept, appreciate, validate and honor yourself, you will also be able to accept, appreciate, validate and honor others. As you validate and honor others, you will learn to validate and honor yourself. Every person you encounter mirrors the way you see yourself. Contemplate your attitudes and beliefs toward yourself

EVERY PERSON YOU ENCOUNTER MIRRORS THE WAY YOU SEE YOURSELF

and then toward others. If you are not accepting, appreciating, validating and honoring yourself or others, see if you are willing to choose to do so. Make a conscious decision now to upgrade your attitudes and beliefs.

9. **PATIENCE/OPENNESS** As you move toward greater inner peace and security, you may experience times of tension, conflict, confusion or turmoil. It is especially important at these times that you are patient with yourself. Patience conveys respect for your own inner process and style and conveys

PATIENCE CONVEYS RESPECT FOR YOUR OWN INNER PROCESS AND STYLE PATIENCE MEANS YOU ARE WILLING TO LET GO OF SELF-CRITICISMS

kindness, compassion and understanding for yourself. Patience means letting go of self-judgments, criticisms and condemnations. It implies self-forgiveness. When you are patient with yourself, you will be more open to exploring yourself, new options and possibilities, more open to deeper feelings and thoughts, and you will be more open to other people. Most important, perhaps, you will be more open to releasing the past and discovering your true Identity in the present. Reflect quietly for a few minutes how you can be more patient and open with yourself and then with others. Write the words "patience" and "openness" on cards and contemplate the significance of these words for your life.

10. **GROWTH/CHANGE** By following the guidelines set out in the previous steps, you will find yourself growing as if a seed had been planted in your mind and is steadily being nurtured. You will find yourself quieting your ego mind, contacting your inner strength, feeling your innocence, accepting and honoring yourself, being more patient and open and developing inner peace and security. As your growth develops, changes will take place, not only within you but also outside you. You may read different books, watch different movies or

AS YOUR GROWTH DEVELOPS, CHANGES
TAKE PLACE WITHIN AND WITHOUT

television shows, associate with different people, or just act differently with the same people. Since inner peace and security will become primary goals, you will make choices and decisions that support these goals and reflect your new attitudes. You may want to change your outer environment to be more peaceful and serene. You may seek out external environments that are aligned with your goals of peace and security. You may want to listen to soothing music, songs or chants that are gentle to your mind and body. Contemplate the growth and change taking place within you. Close your eyes. Breathe deeply. Ask the creative/infinite intelligence within to help you grow and change toward more inner peace and security.

11. **HUMOR/LAUGHTER** As you tap into the source of your inner peace and security, access the place within you of joy, humor and laughter. Lighten up! Take life and yourself less

LIGHTEN UP! TAKE LIFE AND YOURSELF LESS SERIOUSLY

seriously. Begin to look for the humorous side of things, rather than the heavy, important and significant side of everything. By feeling this inner joy, laughing more freely and being more playful, an inner healing will begin to take place. This inner healing will impact positively on the cells and immune system in your body. In other words, inner peace, security and joyfulness all have powerful healing qualities, spiritually, psychologically, emotionally and physically. Laugh more and experience more humor by shifting your perception of events, circumstances and situations in your life and by letting go of the past and the future. Joy, laughter, playfulness and humor are always experienced in the present. Your attitude is the key. Change your attitude and you will enjoy yourself, your relationships and your life more.

YOUR ATTITUDE IS THE KEY

12. **EXTEND/TRANSCEND** Contact the source of your Being once and you will experience inner peace, security, love, joy and strength. It is a natural quality of the Self/Being to extend itself to others. Thus, you will naturally want to share

IT IS A NATURAL QUALITY OF THE SELF/BEING TO EXTEND ITSELF

your peace, security, love, joy and strength. As you extend this quality, you join with the peace and love coming from the Self/Being of other people. This process of extension allows you to transcend the fear and conflict of your "ego" which focuses on "taking and having" and comes from a sense of lack, incompleteness and scarcity. The true experience of your Self/Being is to give, share, join and extend because the nature of the Self/Being within you is wholeness, completeness, peace and love. Transcend the limitations of your ego. Contact your true Identity/Essence. Once again, close your eyes. Breathe deeply. Go within. Ask the infinite/creative intelligence to help you contact your inner Self/Being. Visualize yourself transcending your ego and joining, sharing and extending peace, love and light to others.

Read and frequently reread the twelve steps to creating and developing inner peace and security. Practice the processes and exercises. Gradually, day by day, you will experience more peace and security within your life.

Joan, 28, worked for a publishing firm. She had ulcers, was experiencing emotional distress, and was taking medication. Joan was also unhappy with the amount of responsibility being placed on her at work. She was being asked to take charge of training the entire staff when they converted to a fully computerized system in several months. She learned relaxation and visualization techniques, including the creation and manifestation process, and worked with the "Purpose and Vision in Life" exercise, deciding that her current purpose was to be happy, to have a successful and satisfying career, to have children, and to travel.

When practicing the visualization technique, she would picture herself totally healed, symptom free, anxiety free, peaceful, joyful and confident. She actually saw herself relaxed, happy and smiling. When I asked her to see herself surrounded by a radiant light that traveled through her body from head to toe healing her, Joan would say that she could practically feel the light entering her arteries, muscles, tissues and cells healing everything. She was also able to clearly picture herself going to her work supervisor and expressing her concerns, dissatisfactions and wants and asking specifically for help. Joan was very conscious of making the choice, and of the anticipated benefits. She had no trouble feeling grateful, in advance, for the positive changes she expected to take place.

Finally, she had a discussion with her boss. She requested and received relief from the computer training responsibilities. Soon after this, Joan applied and interviewed for several jobs at other firms in middle management. Within five therapy sessions, she was extremely happy, stress free, free of all medical symptoms and had greatly renewed her self-confidence. The speed of Joan's improvement psychologically, emotionally and physically was unusual. She was very diligent, however, in picturing herself healed and in visualizing herself working in a new, more interesting and exciting job.

Sometimes it is too late to salvage a marriage or relationship but it is never too late to respond to a call for help or love. Such was the case with Rob and Michelle, both in their mid-30's, and married for two years. When Rob came to me, Michelle had recently left him and living nearby with her mother. When I saw Rob, he was clearly distraught, hurt, angry and confused. Michelle agreed to attend the sessions for awhile to see if Rob would change. As she related her part of the story, they had fought most of the two years of their marriage. She no longer felt she loved him. Several months earlier, she had taken a vacation in the Bahamas with her grandmother and met an Austrian man who really attracted her. It had been a long time since she'd felt such joy, affection and peace, she added, though there had been no sexual involvement. The man returned to Austria but they were corresponding regularly. Michelle was thinking of traveling abroad to see him. A few weeks later, she left Rob and moved in with her mother. She said she hadn't felt so content and free of turmoil in years.

Rob wanted Michelle to come back. He pleaded with her. He begged her. He practically commanded her to come back. He said he wanted her and couldn't live without her. When Michelle agreed to attend the therapy sessions, Rob's depression lifted despite the fact that she kept saying she doubted she had any love left for him. They had frequently fought over money, sex, affection, having children and leisure activities. Michelle had once had a brief, sexual encounter with someone else and Rob had become physically violent to her. Occasionally, he drank too much when he was feeling upset. Nevertheless, Rob kept saying over and over that he loved her and needed her. He was desperate.

At first things looked hopeful. Michelle attended the sessions and we worked on improving communication skills. They started to see each other between sessions a few times a week, but Michelle refused to have sex with him. At first, he was patient.

Then he became frustrated. At a party on New Year's Eve, Rob drank too much and became demanding of Michelle. Becoming verbally and physically abusive, he insisted that she spend the night with him at their house. She left the party quickly, hurt and bitter. The next morning, Michelle called her lawyer. She refused to attend any further sessions, claiming that she didn't love Rob anymore and was filing for divorce. Rob became much more depressed, angry, hurt, fearful and confused. His turmoil was intense. He cried a great deal as he experienced a profound sense of grief and loss. No matter what he said or did, Michelle wouldn't see him or talk to him, and wouldn't come to the sessions. His already shaky self-esteem was further eroded and he felt demoralized.

I listened to Robert, empathized with him and supported him through his grief. Gradually, I encouraged him to start doing things again. Rob had been coming home from work, lonely, exhausted and depressed, crying to himself; or he would go to bars and drink. We slowly worked on reframing the dark, gloomy, negative perceptions he had about the end of the relationship into more positive, uplifting and healing perceptions and attitudes.

With my help, Rob practiced the "letting go and releasing" exercises. For example, I taught him the "balloon and garbage can" visual imagery exercise:

1. Visualize yourself dumping all your anger, hurt, sorrow, guilt, pain, negative attitudes and beliefs into a garbage can.

2. Visualize the garbage can attached to a large helium balloon by a long, strong cord. The words on the balloon, in big letters, are "Let Go, Release or Forgive".

3. Watch the helium balloon as it picks up the garbage can with all the "emotional garbage" dumped into it, as it rises higher and higher through the air, through the layers of clouds into interstellar space where it explodes or dissolves into millions of pieces.

During this imagery exercise, Rob found himself releasing all his anger, hurt, depression and judgments toward himself and Michelle. He felt much lighter, more peaceful and uplifted. Rob practiced this exercise often, in addition to reading some recommended self-help books and articles. A peace began to settle over him.

As the grief, sadness, hurt and anger lifted, Rob started to think positively about ending a relationship that hadn't been working anyway. He began to take positive steps toward a new life. He started riding his bike, making plans for a job change and looked into refinancing his house. He was much happier, peaceful, confident and content. He began to seek out and develop new friendships for the first time in his life. Michelle, meanwhile, followed through with the divorce, started to date other men, and reported feeling a deeper sense of peace and security than she'd felt in years.

INNER PEACE/SECURITY
HOME WORK/PLAY SHEET

A. LIST FIVE SHOULDS OR JUDGMENTS ABOUT YOURSELF THAT
    YOU ARE READY AND WILLING TO LET GO:

    1.

    2.

    3.

    4.

    5.

B. LIST FIVE WAYS YOU CAN ACCEPT, APPRECIATE, VALIDATE AND
    HONOR YOURSELF MORE:

    1.

    2.

    3.

    4.

    5.

    OTHERS MORE:

    1.

    2.

    3.

    4.

    5.

C. LIST THREE SITUATIONS IN WHICH YOU CAN BE MORE PATIENT
    AND OPEN WITH YOURSELF OR OTHERS:

    PATIENT   OPEN

    1.   1.

    2.   2.

    3.   3.

THEN LIST THE WORDS "PATIENCE" AND "OPENNESS" ON 3 X 5 CARDS AND CONTEMPLATE THEM EVERY DAY FOR ONE MONTH.

D. REFLECT ON WAYS YOU CAN BE MORE PLAYFUL, JOYFUL AND OF MORE SERVICE TO OTHERS. CLOSE YOUR EYES AND ASK THE CREATIVE/INFINITE INTELLIGENCE, THE DIVINE/HOLY SPIRIT TO HELP YOU. LIST THREE AREAS OF YOUR LIFE WHERE YOU CAN DO THIS:

1.

2.

3.

NOTES:

MORE NOTES

CHAPTER NINE

CREATING AND DEVELOPING AFFECTIONATE, LOVING RELATIONSHIPS

Your ability to create and develop affectionate, loving relationships will greatly improve if you follow these twelve guidelines.

1. **PEACE/SECURITY** You can create a high level of well-being in your intimate relationships by first contacting the inner peace and inner security which dwell within you at the core of your Being/Self. Peace and security cannot be found outside yourself in relationships, achievements, money or success. Learn how to quiet your mind and relax, and you will then feel safe and secure within yourself. This allows you to create a safe, secure environment for your partner. As you quiet your "ego" mind, you will discover a deep reservoir of inner strength and freedom that is invaluable to you in your loving relationships. In the process of doing this, learn how to be gentle and compassionate with yourself so you can be gentle and compassionate with your partner. As you learn to accept, appreciate, validate and honor yourself more, you will

BE GENTLE AND COMPASSIONATE WITH YOURSELF
SO YOU CAN BE GENTLE AND COMPASSIONATE
WITH YOUR PARTNER

be able to do the same for your spouse/lover. The more patience and openness you allow yourself, the more peace and security you will have and the more your heart and mind will open to the deep affection and love within you.

2   **AFFECTION/LOVE**   To create an affectionate, loving relationship, open your heart to the deep caring within you. The heart-centered response to your partner involves being

OPEN YOUR HEART TO THE DEEP CARING WITHIN YOU
BE KIND AND THOUGHTFUL OF YOUR PARTNER'S
NEEDS, WANTS AND DESIRES

kind, thoughtful and understanding of their needs, wants and desires. This requires sensitivity on your part to the non-verbal as well as the verbal messages they send.   Sometimes your partner will want to be hugged, to have their back rubbed, or to take a walk around the block. Sometimes they will want encouragement, a receptive ear, a tender word, a good laugh, or an evening at the movies, dining or dancing. Your tone of voice, interest, touch, and availability all convey affection and love as long as they come from the heart. A romantic evening or afternoon, a sexual embrace, or a surprise gift of flowers can all communicate warmth, caring and tenderness. When you give love and affection, you feel it within. What you give is what you receive. Reflect on how you can give your partner more love and affection today, this week, this month. Then act on it.

3. **AIM/PHILOSOPHY**   In order to have a successful, long-term, intimate relationship, it's best if you and your partner agree on similar aims, philosophy and purpose in life.   Your

vision of what is important to you, your long-range dreams and goals can be aligned with those of your partner. There may be some specific differences in interests or friendships,

YOUR VISION OF WHAT IS IMPORTANT CAN BE
ALIGNED WITH YOUR PARTNER'S

however, the overall agreement level on basic values, aims, purpose and philosophy should be high if the relationship is going to survive, be satisfying, growth-enhancing, enjoyable and effective. Reflect for a few minutes on your basic aims, philosophy, purpose, vision, dreams and values. Share these with your partner and have them share theirs with you. If there are discrepancies, discuss them, listen and share openly and caringly. See if you can gently move into greater alignment and harmony.

4. **REGARD/EMPATHY**   In order to have a lasting, loving relationship, you both will need to have a high degree of regard and liking for each other. To genuinely appreciate and respect each other is the cornerstone of a loving, intimate relationship. To maintain this over time, first learn to appreciate, respect and esteem yourself. Now, by appreciating, respecting and regarding your partner, it will be easier to show empathy and compassion for him/her. Love and caring are most profoundly expressed through empathic responses to feelings, concerns, wants, intentions, desires and dreams. Empathy is an attitude and a feeling. An empathic response is a skill you can learn with an open mind, a caring heart, and a little willingness. Contemplate ways you can express more

EMPATHY IS AN ATTITUDE AND A FEELING
AN EMPATHIC RESPONSE IS A SKILL

positive regard, appreciation, respect and esteem for your partner. Reflect on ways you can be more empathic to his/her feelings, thoughts, desires, dreams and concerns. Ask the creative/infinite intelligence (divine/holy spirit or energy) within to help. Then act on this is a positive, loving way.

5. **NURTURANCE/CONSIDERATION** Learn to be more nurturant to yourself and your partner. When you nurture your spouse/lover, you nourish the growth of the relationship as well as your own growth. One way to nurture your partner is to show compassion for her/his struggles and needs. Another way is to be quick to forgive mistakes, oversights, errors and

YOU CAN NURTURE YOUR PARTNER THROUGH FORGIVENESS AND COMPASSION

peculiarities. This requires patience, thoughtfulness, understanding and trust as well as forgiveness and compassion. The more you are patient, thoughtful and considerate with yourself, the easier it will be for you to do this with your partner. Letting go of judgments and criticisms of yourself and your partner will help a great deal. Close your eyes. Relax. Breathe deeply. See if you are willing to be more nurturant and considerate of yourself and your partner. Choose to do so. If necessary, modify your beliefs and attitudes. You can do it! Visualize yourself giving and then receiving more nurturance and consideration in a loving, caring, compassionate way.

6. **HONESTY/TRUTHFULNESS** You can deepen the level of intimacy and trust in your loving relationships by willingly being more honest and truthful with your own feelings, thoughts, beliefs, attitudes, intentions, desires and dreams. This is an essential ingredient. Be clearer about your aims, philosophy, purpose and vision in life so you can share them with your partner. You will need to take responsibility for creating your own feelings, beliefs, wants and intentions so you can let go of blame and attack. Balance your honest and truthful sharing of thoughts and feelings with compassion,

kindness and caring for your partner. Now, contemplate ways you can be more honest and truthful, first with yourself

*BALANCE YOUR HONEST AND TRUTHFUL SHARING
WITH KINDNESS AND CARING*

and then with your partner. Ask the creative/infinite intelligence within how you can express this honesty and truthfulness in the most loving and constructive way.

7. **LISTENING/EXPRESSING** Being a more effective, empathic listener will improve the quality of your relationship. Listening in an intimate relationship means to listen with your heart, not just your ears, listening with the intent to understand the point of view, frame of reference, and feelings

*LISTEN WITH YOUR HEART, NOT JUST YOUR EARS
LISTEN WITH THE INTENT TO UNDERSTAND*

of your partner. Then feed that understanding back in a clear, compassionate way. This will bring you closer together and deepen your feelings of love for each other. Learn how to express yourself in a clear, direct, non-blaming

*LEARN HOW TO EXPRESS YOURSELF
IN A CLEAR, DIRECT, NON-BLAMING WAY*

way. Practice expressing your feelings, thoughts, beliefs, intentions, expectations, wants, dreams and visions thoughtfully, concisely and non-judgmentally. Take responsibility for your own inner experiences, attitudes, desires, purposes and actions. Then share these with your partner. Learn to listen and express yourself non-defensively and with your heart. This will be much easier if you have first practiced forgiving yourself and your partner.

8. **COMMUNICATION/CONFLICT-RESOLUTION** In order to maintain an affectionate, loving relationship, learn

to be an effective communicator. This requires you to develop the positive, caring attitudes listed in Guidelines 1 through 6, plus the skills of listening and expressing in Guideline 7, plus conflict-resolution skills. Most conflicts arising in a loving relationship can be resolved by listening, sharing and forgiving. However, some conflicts require problem-solving skills that start with developing a positive attitude. First, define the problem clearly and specifically. Discuss one problem at a time. Next, generate a list of creative alternatives. Then discuss these alternatives with the attitude of finding a mutually acceptable, peaceful and beneficial solution. Before starting this process, you may

DEFINE THE PROBLEM CLEARLY.
DISCUSS ONE PROBLEM AT A TIME.
GENERATE A LIST OF CREATIVE ALTERNATIVES.
ASK FOR INNER GUIDANCE

close your eyes and relax. During a period of silence, meditation or prayer, call upon the creative/infinite intelligence within for guidance and resourcefulness. Following these steps carefully will maximize your coping responses. Finally, you and your partner will want to evaluate the success of the solutions you have implemented. Reflect now on ways you can communicate more effectively while learning to problem-solve in a meaningful, peaceful and mutually beneficial way.

9. **CREATIVITY/ADAPTABILITY** From the two previous guidelines, you can see that creativity and flexibility are important for the skills of finding alternatives and generating possible solutions to problems. In order to be creative and flexible, learn to quiet your "ego" mind, relax and go within to the source of your creativity, your true Self/Being. When you are angry, hurt, tense and upset, you are much less likely to be able to access this creative resource. Enhanced

creativity and flexibility allow you to be more adaptable in your intimate relationships. This allows you and your partner

ENHANCED CREATIVITY AND FLEXIBILITY
ALLOW YOU TO BE MORE ADAPTABLE

to make changes internally and externally to changing circumstances. Births, deaths, relocations, job changes, children arriving and leaving, illnesses and other situations require you to be adaptable and open to change. In many cases you will want to use resources in a flexible way, not only within your immediate family, but also within your personal, community and spiritual network. Contemplate ways to be more creative, flexible and adaptable in your intimate relationships. Close your eyes and picture yourself making the necessary changes to deepen the effectiveness and lovingness of your relationships with your spouse/lover.

10. **COHESIVENESS/PRIVACY** You will discover that a loving relationship requires times of cohesiveness (togetherness) and times of privacy. When you are together, you can share your thoughts and feelings, problem-solve, be affectionate or sexually intimate, go to the movies, watch television, eat meals at home together, socialize with friends, or spend time with your immediate family. Personal and often spiritual growth require that you have enough time alone or with friends to nurture other aspects of yourself. With friends, you can share interests, hobbies, ideas, support and caring. You need time to be alone, to have your own privacy, and to nourish friendships. Encourage your partner to have private time alone and with friends, too. First, however, dialogue,

DIALOGUE AND NEGOTIATE WITH YOUR PARTNER
TO FIND THE OPTIMAL BALANCE BETWEEN
COHESIVENESS AND PRIVACY,
TOGETHERNESS AND BEING ALONE

share and negotiate with your partner to find the optimal balance between cohesiveness and privacy, togetherness and being alone. When that optimal level is reached and you have also followed Guidelines 1-9, you will experience a profound level of companionship, friendship and emotional support that will develop when you are together and be experienced when you are apart.

11. **LIGHTNESS/FUN** Enjoy your relationship with your partner a lot more by lightening up, laughing and playing. By becoming less serious, heavy or task-oriented, you introduce

LAUGH, PLAY, LIGHTEN UP AND
ENJOY YOUR PARTNER MORE

lightness into your life and your relationships. By allowing yourself to be more humorous and playful, you experience more joy and fun. You both will discover that humor, play and fun make problems seem less important and more easily resolved. Discover that joy is a central quality of your Self/Being and can deepen and nurture your love for each other by allowing you to enjoy each other and life more. Sometimes it's best to first let go of beliefs and attitudes, concerning sinfulness, wrong-doing, failure, blame and guilt, or to lighten up on your drive for success and achievement. Allow yourself, now, to have fun with your spouse/lover; allow yourself to feel the joy, lightness, compassion and love developing, expanding and deepening as you do.

12. **LOYALTY/DEVOTION** When you stay in a successful, loving, affectionate relationship for a long period of time, 15 years or more, certain qualities will develop that may also appear in briefer relationships. You will be committed not only to your own personal/spiritual growth, but also to your partner's, and the growth of the relationship. You will have made it your intention to make the relationship a caring and

effective one. You will feel loyal and devoted to your partner; i.e., to your partner's health, well-being, growth, success, peace, joy and love. Your loyalty and devotion can develop to the point of feeling profound sacredness and

YOUR LOYALTY AND DEVOTION CAN DEVELOP INTO SACREDNESS AND GRATITUDE

gratitude to your partner. Eventually the loyalty and devotion will develop into a deeper level of unity between you, coming from your Self/Being as you mutually support and enhance the individual, relationship and spiritual growth of each other. Reflect on your current relationship with your partner. Contemplate ways you can deepen the commitment, loyalty and devotion, even the sacredness, gratitude and unity of your loving relationship. Choose to enhance the quality of well-being. Visualize it. Feel the joy, affection and love as it grows and expands.

Reread the twelve guidelines for an affectionate, loving relationship often. Contemplate the ideas and suggestions. Shift your perceptions and attitudes. Act on the ideas. Gradually, and sometimes dramatically, you will find the quality of your relationship growing and transforming. Then you will feel even greater love, peace and joy than ever before.

Bill came to me at the urging of his 22 year old girlfriend, Sherri. He was 23 at the time and had an intense temper. Although he said he loved Sherri, his anger and frustration seemed to override any pleasure he received from the relationship. Moreover, they were to be married in three months. I saw the two of them together for the first interview. Sherri was very attractive and appeared to be more intelligent than Bill. I must confess that I wondered to myself why Sherri even stayed with Bill, let alone wanted to marry him. Bill was extremely jealous and the slightest indication that Sherri was paying attention to someone else, even girlfriends or her parents, could upset him. If Sherri was ten minutes late for a date, Bill would feel extremely hurt and go into a rage, screaming, shouting and calling her names. Nevertheless, they wanted to get married and the wedding date was set. I had less than three months to facilitate the healing process for Bill, and between Bill and Sherri. Sherri said she'd break the engagement and end the relationship if we didn't succeed. Needless to say, Bill was very motivated, despite internal blocks and obstacles to change.

As I do with all my clients, I helped Bill get clear about his purpose and vision in life and his short and long-range goals. His primary focus was to enhance his self worth and peace of mind and to improve his relationship with Sherri. I related to Bill several success stories of other clients who, with the right motivation, right focus, clear-cut goals, willingness, strong determination and persistence, were able to make rapid changes in their lives. I pointed out that Bill's anger was connected to the unreasonable expectations he had for Sherri, the faulty judgments he made about her and himself, his shaky self-esteem and the perfectionistic standards he held for everyone, including himself. We discussed a simplified model I sometimes use.

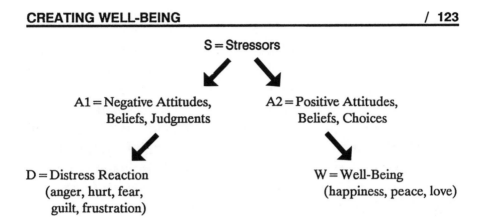

The S in the model represents the external stressors in one's life; A1 equals the negative attitudes, beliefs, judgments, perceptions, expectations and thoughts; A2 equals positive attitudes, beliefs, choices, perceptions, thoughts and expectations; D equals any emotional distress reaction such as anger, hurt, fear, guilt, frustration, shame or depression; and W equals well being; i.e., any happiness, peace, love, joy or excitement. I call this the S.A.D. - S.A.W. Model.

I then explained to Bill that distress reactions (D) are never based on the external stressors (S), but on the intervening negative attitudes, perceptions, beliefs, expectations and thoughts (A1). Moreover, if he learned to identify the A1's and then substitutes positive attitudes, perceptions, beliefs, judgments, expectations and thoughts (A2's), he could move gradually from distressing (D) emotional reactions to emotional reactions of (W) well-being. Bill was also told that he could call upon the creative/infinite intelligence within him to help him.

At first Bill's progress was slow. Even I began to doubt that he could make the necessary changes within such a short time. I told him to try to be gentler with himself and Sherri, to practice patience, and to allow himself to be more accepting and loving. After one month, these commendations started to catch on and I felt myself silently cheering Bill on. He started to become angry and jealous less often and got over it more quickly. He began to be much more aware of his negative self-talk and gradually started to substitute positive self-talk more frequently.

I encouraged Bill to start listening to Sherri with his heart and not just his ears and to begin to see things from her point of view. This training in empathic listening enabled him to gradually become more compassionate toward Sherri. I also taught him how to express his feelings more clearly and directly in a non-blaming way. As a result, he and Sherri were able to have more meaningful, useful and less heated conversations. Eventually we discussed ways to problem-solve and resolve conflicts by generating and discussing alternatives and looking for and finding mutually beneficial solutions to problems. Bill discovered that with positive self-talk and a positive mental attitude, he was able to increasingly implement these problem-solving methods. Of course, it was awkward for him at first as it usually is when learning new skills and attitudes, but the benefits were very substantial. During this process, he learned to appreciate and respect himself and Sherri, and to see the highest and best in each other rather than the worst. Relaxation and visualization exercises also helped to calm his emotions and focus his mind. Sherri appreciated even the small, positive changes and started to encourage and reinforce him. His progress accelerated and he started to feel calmer, noticing that there were days when he didn't get upset or angry at all. As he shifted his perceptions and attitudes, he started to love Sherri even more and to like himself more. Naturally I encouraged, supported, nurtured and guided him in this process and reinforced positive changes in a loving way. In the meantime, I was also aware that "what you teach, you learn, and what you focus on expands and strengthens", so I was also clearly benefiting as well from this process. Over the three months we had therapy sessions, Bill's stress, anger and anxiety level dropped dramatically and his self-esteem and well-being level improved markedly along with his relationship with Sherri. She joined us for the last session, two weeks before the wedding, was very happy with the relationship and was as eager as Bill to marry, which they did.

AFFECTIONATE/LOVING RELATIONSHIPS HOME WORK/PLAY SHEET

A. LIST FIVE WAYS YOU CAN (AND WILL) GIVE YOUR PARTNER MORE LOVE AND AFFECTION.

1.

2.

3.

4.

5.

B. LIST TWO AREAS IN WHICH YOU AND YOUR PARTNER SHARE SIMILAR AIMS, PHILOSOPHY, PURPOSE, VISION, DREAMS AND VALUES.

1.

2.

THEN LIST TWO AREAS WHERE YOU DIFFER.

1.

2.

DISCUSS THESE AREAS OF SIMILARITY AND DIFFERENCE WITH YOUR PARTNER. SHARE LOVINGLY AND LISTEN WITH YOUR HEART. SEE IF YOU CAN MOVE INTO GREATER ALIGNMENT.

C. WRITE DOWN THREE WAYS YOU CAN EXPRESS MORE POSITIVE REGARD, ESTEEM, APPRECIATION AND RESPECT FOR YOUR PARTNER.

1.

2.

3.

AND THREE WAYS YOU CAN BE MORE EMPATHIC TO HIS/HER FEELINGS, THOUGHTS, DESIRES, DREAMS AND CONCERNS.

1.

2.

3.

ASK THE CREATIVE/INFINITE INTELLIGENCE (THE DIVINE/HOLY SPIRIT OR ENERGY WITHIN YOU) FOR HELP. YOU CAN DO IT!

D. LIST THREE AREAS IN WHICH YOU CAN NURTURE YOUR PARTNER MORE.

1.

2.

3.

E. LIST TWO AREAS WHERE YOU CAN BE MORE HONEST AND TRUTH-FUL.

WITH YOURSELF   YOUR PARTNER

1.   1.

2.   2.

ASK THE CREATIVE/INFINITE INTELLIGENCE WITHIN YOU HOW YOU CAN EXPRESS THIS HONESTY AND TRUTHFULNESS IN THE MOST LOVING AND CONSTRUCTIVE WAY.

F. LIST THREE AREAS WHERE YOU NEED TO FORGIVE YOUR PARTNER.

1.

2.

3.

THEN LIST THREE AREAS WHERE YOU NEED TO LISTEN BETTER WITH YOUR HEART TO YOUR PARTNER (AND FEEDBACK EMPATHI-CALLY WHAT YOU HAVE HEARD).

1.

2.

3.

THEN LIST THREE AREAS WHERE YOU CAN EXPRESS YOURSELF MORE DIRECTLY AND CLEARLY IN A NON-BLAMING WAY.

1.

2.

3.

G. THEN USE THE SEVEN STEP, PROBLEM-SOLVING PROCESS FOR MORE EFFECTIVE AND LOVING COMMUNICATION IN YOUR IN-TIMATE RELATIONSHIPS.
   1. QUIET YOUR MIND, BREATHE DEEPLY AND RELAX.
   2. ASK THE CREATIVE/INFINITE INTELLIGENCE WITHIN FOR INNER GUIDANCE AND RESOURCEFULNESS.
   3. CLEARLY DEFINE THE PROBLEM WITH YOUR PARTNER.
   4. GENERATE A LIST OF CREATIVE ALTERNATIVES.
   5. DISCUSS THE ALTERNATIVES WITH THE ATTITUDE OF FINDING A MUTUALLY ACCEPTABLE, PEACEFUL AND BENEFICIAL SOLUTION.
   6. IMPLEMENT THE AGREED UPON SOLUTION.
   7. EVALUATE THE SUCCESS OF THE SOLUTION.

REPEAT STEPS 1 THROUGH 7 FOR EACH PROBLEM UNTIL A MUTUALLY BENEFICIAL SOLUTION IS ATTAINED. YOU CAN DO IT!

H. LIST TWO AREAS WHERE YOU CAN BE MORE FLEXIBLE IN YOUR INTIMATE RELATIONSHIP.

1.

2.

THEN LIST THREE AREAS WHERE YOU CAN FLEXIBLY USE RESOURCES WITHIN YOUR EXTENDED FAMILY, PERSONAL, COM-MUNITY OR SPIRITUAL NETWORK TO HELP YOU SOLVE PROBLEMS WITH YOUR PARTNER.

1.

2.

3.

I. WRITE DOWN TWO WAYS YOU LIKE TO BE WITH YOUR PARTNER AND TWO WAYS YOU LIKE TO BE ALONE.

TOGETHER   ALONE

1.   1.

2.   2.

THEN SHARE AND DISCUSS WITH YOUR PARTNER, SEARCHING FOR AN OPTIMAL BALANCE FOR BOTH OF YOU.

J. LIST THREE WAYS YOU AND YOUR PARTNER CAN HAVE MORE FUN TOGETHER.

1.

2.

3.

K. WRITE DOWN FIVE AREAS WHERE YOU FEEL ESPECIALLY GRATE-FUL TO YOUR PARTNER.

1.

2.

3.

4.

5.

AND FIVE AREAS WHERE YOU FEEL ESPECIALLY LOYAL AND DEVOTED TO YOUR PARTNER.

1.

2.

3.

4.

5.

NOTES:

CHAPTER TEN

CREATING AND DEVELOPING CARING, CLOSE FRIENDSHIPS IN LIFE

Use these twelve steps to guide you in creating and developing caring, close friendships. You will find your life greatly enriched and your well being substantially enhanced.

1. **AFFECTION/LOVE** You can learn to create friendships that have many of the same qualities as affectionate, loving relationships. Close friendships require appreciation and respect, which occurs when you have positive regard, liking and esteem for another. Your values, beliefs, attitudes and

    CLOSE FRIENDSHIPS REQUIRE APPRECIATION AND RESPECT

    expectations influence who you appreciate, regard and esteem. Learn to broaden your interests so you will have more in common with different people. Let go of judgments and biases and thereby increase your liking, respect, affection, understanding and even love for more people. As you do this, more people will become your friends. See the inner light and goodness in all people and discover the uniqueness, the beauty in every person. Then you will discover that every

*SEE THE INNER LIGHT, BEAUTY, GOODNESS
AND UNIQUENESS IN ALL PEOPLE*

person is a potential friend, someone from whom you can learn and be enriched. You will discover that everyone you meet is your mirror reflecting your attitude and conscious-ness in all your relationships. Choose to see everyone as your friend and your teacher.

2. **CARING/CLOSENESS** Caring is central to developing friendships. This means to appreciate and respect, feel affec-tion towards, be interested in, look forward to times spent

*CARING IS CENTRAL TO DEVELOPING
FRIENDSHIPS*

together, and even to love. Caring is a feeling that is easily reciprocated. Closeness comes from caring. When you truly care about someone, you feel closer to them. When you care about them and they care about you, you become more open, vulnerable, and willing to be part of their lives. As the caring and openness deepens, the relationship deepens; perhaps you think of each other often or you just feel a very warm and special place in your heart for that person. For some, the caring grows into love that becomes unconditional.

3. **ACCEPT/PROTECT** Caring, close relationships require ac-ceptance. Central to this kind of relationships is the willing-ness to accept each unique other as they are and let go of

*CARING, CLOSE RELATIONSHIPS
REQUIRE ACCEPTANCE*

criticisms as much as possible. The more you are able to ac-cept yourself and let go of judgments and criticisms toward yourself, the more you will be able to accept another person in a friendship. Close, caring friendships, based on acceptance, frequently bring out protective feelings in the people involved. You don't want any harm or even slight hurt to come to that person. You accept them and want to protect them from extremely difficult or painful experiences. Although you know they are ultimately responsible for their own life, you empathize with the distress they feel, accept them, and often desire to protect them from further distress.

4. **SHARE/CONFIDE** Not every friendship serves the same purpose or function. Most of your caring, close friendships will be based on a willingness and desire to share interests, ideas, feelings, or activities. Sharing is central to most close friendships. It generates a feeling of joining and connectedness, while increasing trust and acceptance. The more you learn to share and confide, the deeper and more meaningful

SHARING AND CONFIDING LEAD TO DEEPER
AND MORE MEANINGFUL FRIENDSHIPS

your friendship will become. Being able to confide is a valuable function of a friendship. It helps to reduce tension, anxiety, depression, anger and other unpleasant emotions. It can invigorate you. As you share and confide in a friend who accepts and cares about you, you feel nurtured and appreciated. As you empathically listen to a friend's sharing and confiding, they feel nurtured and appreciated. Deepen your friendships by more sharing, confiding and listening.

5. **SUPPORT/COMFORT** A close, caring friend is someone you can count on for support and someone you naturally feel like supporting in a variety of ways: listening to them, going places, eating out, exchanging ideas, hobbies and interests, fixing something, hugging or crying on their shoulder. Although physical, economic and intellectual support are fre-

quently given and valuable in friendships, the most satisfying support is usually emotional. When you give comfort and receive comfort, give support and receive support, you feel less alone and isolated. You feel comforted and supported

> *WHEN YOU GIVE AND RECEIVE SUPPORT*
> *AND COMFORT*
> *YOU FEEL LESS ALONE*

in the universe. Close your eyes. Relax. Breathe deeply. Go within. Ask the creative/infinite intelligence within you how you can develop closer, caring friendships based on affection, respect, sharing, supporting and comforting. Choose to create it for yourself. Visualize it happening. Anticipate all the positive benefits to you.

6. **CLARIFY/CATALYZE** Some friends help clarify your thinking, ideas, feelings, plans, decisions and anticipated actions. They may also let you be a source of clarification for them. Clarification frequently brings not only clarity, but also understanding, wisdom and renewed self-confidence. Some friends serve as a catalyst for new beliefs, attitudes, decisions and actions. These can range from changing a hairstyle or a

> *SOME FRIENDS HELP CLARIFY YOUR*
> *THINKING AND FEELINGS*
> *SOME FRIENDS SERVE AS A CATALYST*
> *FOR NEW ATTITUDES OR ACTIONS*

job, taking a vacation in an unusual place, expressing your true feelings, learning how to like yourself more, or exploring a new spiritual path. Certain friends may introduce you to new ideas or alternatives, or just suggest that you take some new steps or actions. By their interest in some topic or area, they may facilitate re-examining your point of view, attitudes and actions. You, of course, can also serve as a catalyst to your friends. Reflect for a few minutes on which of your friends has served as a clarifier and catalyst in your life. Then contemplate for whom you have served as a clarifier and catalyst.

7. **ENCOURAGE/UPLIFT** Some close friends will encourage you when you are discouraged and uplift you when you feel dispirited just as you will often do for them. Learn to be a better friend by focusing on the inner qualities of beauty, strength, competence and goodness in your friends. Then,

> *LEARN TO BE A BETTER FRIEND BY FOCUSING ON THE INNER QUALITIES OF BEAUTY STRENGTH, COMPETENCE AND GOODNESS IN YOUR FRIENDS*

even when your friend is dejected or disappointed at some setback, you can point out their positive qualities and abilities and help shift their perception from so-called "defeats" to new possibilities and opportunities. Listen, support, nurture and encourage them to keep going, try again, persist. Reassure them, or joke with them, or tell them how much you care about, appreciate or respect them. You can acknowledge their competencies and skills and be a beacon of light amidst the temporary darkness and gloom. Select some friends who do this for you. For a few minutes, contemplate ways in which you can encourage and uplift your friends.

8. **ASSIST/HELP** There are times in a close, caring friendship when you will be called upon to assist or when you will need assistance. You may assist by giving someone a ride, lending them an audio/video cassette, a magazine to read, babysitting, knitting their baby a sweater, making a phone call, or helping them to run a workshop. They may do the same thing for you. Sometimes they experience an emergency or crisis in their lives (illness, death, separation, job loss, accident). A good friend is there not only for listening, supporting, clarify-

ing, encouraging and uplifting, but also with material or physical assistance or a hug. Every communication by a friend can be perceived at one level as either a communication of love and caring, or a call for help, love and caring.

EVERY COMMUNICATION BY A FRIEND
IS EITHER A SHARING OF CARING AND LOVE
OR A CALL FOR HELP, CARING AND LOVE

Consequently, when a friend appears to be upset or angry with you, learn to see it as a call for help, caring or love. Reflect on ways you have given and received assistance and help. Contemplate further ways you can be of more assistance and help in a concerned, caring way.

9. **ADVISE/PROBLEM-SOLVE** You will spend more time with some friends because of the common interests you share. You confide in other friends or pour your troubles out to them. Some you seek out because you want their advice, or they will seek you out because they want your advice. The advice might have to do with important emotional, psychological or spiritual issues in your life. Good friends help each other problem-solve by clarifying the nature of the

GOOD FRIENDS HELP EACH OTHER
PROBLEM-SOLVE

problem, helping each other explore the alternatives to solving the problem, evaluating the alternatives, selecting a workable solution, and dealing with strong feelings that often arise during this process. The different perspective and frame of reference provided by a close, caring friend can be valuable in a friendship when they are clearly requested. Reflect on your friendships. When do you give or receive helpful, constructive advice and problem-solving assistance?

10. **QUESTION/CHALLENGE** Some friends can serve another important function in your life; to question your way of thinking, your ideas, beliefs, attitudes, decisions, actions and, at times, even your feelings. For this to be successful and maintain the friendship, you need to have a trusting, solid relationship. If this type of relationship exists, it can stimulate you to experience greater levels of creativity, clearer thinking, wiser decision-making, and more meaningful relationships. Sometimes friends can serve to challenge your excuses, blaming, biases, denials of responsibility, procrastination, guilt, anger and fear. You, of course, can do this for close friends. Most often, questioning and challenging will need to be done gently and lovingly and even then with only one or two of your closest friends or it will be perceived as judgmental and critical rather than supportive and nurturing. You may, however,

QUESTIONING AND CHALLENGING WILL NEED
TO BE DONE GENTLY AND LOVINGLY

find that you seek certain friends or they seek you just for this purpose. For a few minutes, contemplate which friends you question and challenge and which question and challenge you. Is it helpful and constructive? Is it gentle and caring?

11. **REMINISCE/DREAM** There are occasions when you will spend most of your time reminiscing with a friend about the past. This serves as a kind of joining and bonding and revives memories, usually warm but sometimes distressing. You may have buddies from your high school or college, camp or service days with whom you do little else but reminisce about the "good old days". Affection, companionship, empathy and caring are stimulated by these exchanges. At other times, you seek out friends (or they seek you out) because they encourage you to dream, explore or pursue your wildest ideas,

fantasies and ambitions about the future. They encourage
you to "go for it"; whatever you desire the most, whatever your

SOME FRIENDS WILL ENCOURAGE YOU TO DREAM,
TO EXPLORE, AND TO GO FOR IT

most cherished dreams of success, excitement, daring and ad-
venture. Sometimes the guidance given by these friends will
need to be moderated later by more "reality-oriented"
friends. Yet there are times when this is exactly what you
want or need to support and stimulate you to do something
you always wanted to do. Reflect on those with whom you
dream or reminisce. Close your eyes. Relax. Breathe slowly and deeply. Ask the creative/infinite intelligence within
what reminiscences from the past and what dreams for the
future are most aligned with your highest good.

12. **PLAY/ENJOY** You will discover that there are some friends
with whom you will love to just play. These friends have a
great sense of humor and are always looking on the joyful side
of things. Whenever you are discouraged or dejected, they
can make you laugh. Perhaps they clown around, make jokes,
tickle you, fool around or act silly. It doesn't matter. You
just know that with them you enjoy yourself, laugh more, feel
lighter and uplifted. You can do this for others. As you give,
so you receive. You may have some friends with whom you
can even alternate sharing, confiding, assisting and helping,
and then at other times, just playing and enjoying. Humor,
joy, laughter and play are essential parts of friendship and

HUMOR, JOY, LAUGHTER AND PLAY
ARE ESSENTIAL PARTS OF FRIENDSHIP

contribute greatly to enhancing well-being and health.
Reflect on ways you can increase your sense of play and en-
joyment in your relationships. Close your eyes. Relax. Ask

the creative/infinite intelligence (the divine/holy spirit or energy) to help you to do this. Try it now.

Reread the twelve sets of characteristics and guidelines for creating and developing caring, close friendships. Focus on them. Contemplate them. Then begin to act. Gradually, though sometimes dramatically, you will find the quality and/or quantity of your meaningful, nurturing friendships growing and expanding.

Virginia was 35 years old when she first came to see me. Living for several years with her long-time friend Mary, she was working full-time in a bank in her first full-time job, and part-time in a book store. She was cute, soft-spoken, intense, and very fastidious and precise in her work. Her relationship with Mary, her roommate, was becoming increasingly more upsetting and frustrating. Mary's father had recently died and Mary was spending every weekend with her mother. Previously, Virginia and Mary had spent a great deal of time together on weekends going to movies, shopping and eating out. Virginia felt alone, isolated, neglected and resentful, but wasn't sharing her feelings with Mary. Mary, in turn, said very little and what she did say, Virginia often didn't want to hear. Communication was poor and deteriorating every week. The sensitive and tender moments that Virginia and Mary used to spend together were infrequent now. Mary was talking about moving in with her mother and leaving Virginia. This was an even greater threat to Virginia.

Virginia was also upset about her relationship with a co-worker at the bookstore, with a former friend, and with her parents who had frequent, bitter marital arguments. To make matters worse, Virginia was beginning to feel increasingly dissatisfied in her job as she was being criticized for doing things differently. Naturally, she felt her way was better and more efficient. It was immediately clear that Virginia was feeling hurt, resentful, disappointed, frustrated and confused.

Despite all her difficulties, Virginia had a gentleness, kindness and genuineness to her that I liked right away. She was truly motivated to find a solution to her multiple problems. I explained to her that every time someone (friend, parent, colleague, employer) was angry at her, it was a signal that underneath that person felt hurt and fearful and was calling for help and love. This helped her to reframe and re-perceive the problem and the solution. Virginia wanted love, affection, caring and communication from other people that she wasn't currently receiving, or at least not in the form she wanted. Most likely, this originally stemmed from her lack of a nurturing relationship with her mother and father. Now, however, it indicated Virginia didn't love herself sufficiently and was judging herself and others in her life. She was unforgiving and had exceedingly high expectations for herself and those in relationships with her. Virginia also didn't communicate her feelings clearly and directly and didn't sufficiently offer love, care, concern and respect to others. This information was given gradually and empathically over time and in a nurturing, supportive way.

Virginia accepted these explanations and gradually started to put them into effect in her life. I also taught her several relaxation/meditation and visualization exercises, including the creation and manifestation process and the forgiveness imagery exercises (see Chapter Two and Three). At first her relationship with Mary became worse as she shared her feelings about the relationship. They continued, however, to be friends. Expectations lowered in the relationship and resentment and hurt feelings decreased. Virginia forgave Mary and felt more warmth and compassion toward her. They started to do more things together and to communicate more. As they began to feel more positive and affectionate toward each other, the friendship deepened. Once again they liked, respected and supported each other. As this developed, Virginia practiced forgiving her former friend, her colleague at the bookstore, and her mother and father. First her perceptions, attitudes and feelings changed, and then her behavior.

Step by step, Virginia was more empathic, kinder, more thoughtful and more considerate of first, Mary, and then the other important people in her life. All her relationships started to turn around, first from negative to neutral, and then from neutral to positive. Eventually, Virginia started to warmly talk to her mother and to her friend and colleague. Soon after this, Virginia's mother called and told Virginia that following a big battle with her husband, her minister had given her the same posi- tive, uplifting advice Virginia had been giving her. Her mother then openly acknowledged, appreciated and expressed her grate- fulness to Virginia. Virginia had taught her mother what she had learned from working out her relationship with Mary.

Virginia's tension and dissatisfaction at work increased for some time. Following an unexpectedly critical six month evalua- tion, she saw no positive future for herself. More confident now that she had greatly improved her relationship with Mary, she decided to change jobs and complete her Master's degree. We discussed this at some length. Virginia then visualized what she wanted; i.e., a new job and more education. With two weeks, she enrolled in night school and began working toward her degree. She then wrote a marvelous self-recruitment letter to five banks. Two of them called her in for interviews and offered her jobs; one at a substantial raise in pay and responsibility. Three weeks later, she gave notice to her current employer and one month after, she started work at her new job. By that time, she had also trans- formed all of her relationships, was relaxed, peaceful, confident, enthusiastic, and in a very high state of well-being. The whole process took 18 sessions, spread out over nine months. A rebirth had taken place.

FRIENDSHIP
HOME WORK/PLAY SHEET

A. LIST THE NAMES OF FIVE FRIENDS OR ACQUAINTANCES WITH WHOM YOU WOULD LIKE TO SHARE AND CONFIDE:

1.

2.

3.

4.

5.

B. LIST THREE WAYS YOU CAN SUPPORT AND COMFORT OTHERS MORE:

1.

2.

3.

THEN LIST THREE WAYS YOU CAN ENCOURAGE AND UPLIFT OTHERS MORE:

1.

2.

3.

NOTES:

MORE NOTES:

CHAPTER ELEVEN

GENERATING A SENSE OF GRATITUDE AND ABUNDANCE IN LIFE

These twelve guidelines will help you create a sense of gratitude and abundance in life.

1. **CARING/CLOSENESS** Caring, close friendships based on esteem, respect, appreciation and liking develop deep bonds of affection and often love. In order to create these kinds of friendships, learn to accept yourself more so you can be more accepting of your friends. As your acceptance grows and deepens, you will find yourself sharing and confiding openly and listening to your friends do the same. You will give and receive emotional, intellectual and sometimes physical or spiritual support and comfort. Some of your friends will help you clarify your thinking, feelings and actions, or catalyze you to new ways of perceiving, thinking and acting. With most friends, you will uplift them when they are discouraged and they will do the same for you. Giving assistance and guidance in problem-solving are major functions served by close, caring friendships. Some very close friends will question or challenge you to greater growth and self-exploration, while

others will reminisce with you about the past or support you in pursuing dreams for the future. Finally, with some friends you will just play, laugh and have fun. In all cases, you can learn to be grateful for your friends and see them as examples of your abundance in life.

YOU CAN LEARN TO BE GRATEFUL
FOR YOUR FRIENDS

2. **GRATITUDE/ABUNDANCE** A sense of gratitude is a powerful inner experience. When you allow yourself to experience gratitude for all the people, situations and circumstances in your life, you are opening your heart to a great inner treasure. More miracles occur from gratitude (and forgiveness) than from anything else. Love flourishes where there is gratitude (and forgiveness). Choosing to be grateful

MIRACLES OCCUR FROM GRATITUDE
AND FORGIVENESS
LOVE FLOURISHES WHERE THERE IS
GRATITUDE AND FORGIVENESS

for what you have received, experienced, and learned is a marvelous gift you give to others. Choosing to be grateful to your inner or higher Self, to the creative/infinite intelligence, the divine/holy spirit that dwells within you is to open yourself to inner abundance and to the abundance of the universe. Experience this infinite abundance which comes from within you and manifests outside you by allowing yourself to see all the positive things that have already entered your life. To further increase your experience of abundance, choose to be grateful in advance for all the positive, loving, joyous experiences, the prosperity and the blessings that will be coming to you.

3. **THANKFULNESS/APPRECIATION** Feeling grateful is feeling thankful. Every day becomes a day of thanksgiving

when you give thanks to everyone and everything that has been given to you, directly and indirectly. Give thanks for your health, intellect, resources, skills, creativity and love. Give thanks to the creator for the air, water, plants, animals, earth and stars. Give thanks to other people for their support, sharing, nurturance, guidance, love, joy and ideas. Look for opportunities to be thankful and appreciative. What you

LOOK FOR OPPORTUNITIES TO BE
THANKFUL AND APPRECIATIVE

focus on expands. What you concentrate on, you absorb. Appreciating allows you to experience more beauty, goodness, and even the holiness of life. The mind is like a mirror. What you appreciate in others, you will appreciate in yourself, and others will appreciate in you. What you give is what you receive. If you radiate thankfulness and appreciation, that is what you will attract. Thankfulness and appreciation are the two great cornerstones of gratitude and abundance.

4. **REJOICE/CELEBRATE** The more grateful, thankful and appreciative you are, the more you will feel like rejoicing, and an inner joyfulness will well up within you. Radiate gratefulness and you will draw it toward you like a magnet. To fully appreciate and be thankful, allow yourself to experience the abundance of the universe. Joyfulness is a quality of both

RADIATE GRATEFULNESS AND YOU WILL DRAW IT
TOWARD YOU LIKE A MAGNET
JOYFULNESS IS A QUALITY OF BOTH
GRATITUDE AND ABUNDANCE

gratitude and abundance, a link between them. Celebrate and rejoice at what you have given and what you have received. Choose to celebrate and rejoice, in advance, for all the wonderful people, circumstances, events and experiences that you will have in the future. *In this way, you create your own personal reality.*

5. **DEFENSELESS/RECEPTIVE** In order to experience gratitude, choose to be more defenseless. Defensiveness is like a closed fist. It doesn't allow anything new, exciting or wonderful into it. Defenselessness is like an open hand; it is receptive to positive, loving, joyful and prosperous experiences entering into it. This creates a mind and heart receptive to new, joyful experiences, opportunities and beauty. To experience gratitude, thankfulness and appreciation, practice being more open, receptive and defenseless. Learn to re-

PRACTICE BEING MORE OPEN, RECEPTIVE AND DEFENSELESS

ceive more, defend less, and be more attentive to those experiences for which you can be grateful. It requires a shift in perception, a shift in attitude. A little willingness and attentiveness is all that is necessary. As you choose to be more defenseless and more receptive, you will experience more joy, appreciation and abundance in your life.

6. **PRESENCE/CONSCIOUSNESS** As you become less defensive, more receptive and open, you begin to experience a divine presence, your Self/Being within you. This divine presence, the source of your experiences of gratitude, abundance, appreciation, joy and love is also called infinite or pure consciousness. When you go within and contact the divine presence, the infinite consciousness, you will be connecting with the infinite, creative intelligence within you and the universe. This consciousness generates a divine energy that is constantly, eternally and abundantly flowing. Close your

CONSCIOUSNESS GENERATES A DIVINE ENERGY THAT IS ABUNDANTLY FLOWING

eyes. Relax. Breathe deeply. Ask the creative/infinite intelligence, the divine/holy spirit or energy within to help you contact this consciousness which loves you unconditionally. Allow yourself to feel this love. Allow yourself to feel the infinite abundance within you. Allow yourself to feel gratitude for contacting your Self/Being.

7. **SUFFICIENCY/SUPPLY** This infinite presence or consciousness is complete, whole and sufficient. When you contact the source of your Self/Being, you contact the energy source of total sufficiency within you and the universe. This energy of all-pervasive sufficiency is always working on your behalf to meet all your needs and desires which are for your highest good. You can choose to align yourself with this energy. Visualize a white light entering your head. As the white light slowly flows through your entire body, feel yourself enveloped in a radiant, protective, healing and all-sufficient energy. Within this light is also the infinite supply which exists within you and the universe. It is all-pervasive, fully conscious, and always active. Release all barriers to experiencing this. These blocks consist of feelings or beliefs of lack, emptiness, fear, negativity or separation from your source of infinite supply or sufficiency. Repeat the following affirmation: "I rejoice and give thanks for the ever-flowing, always abundant source of infinite supply, sufficiency, blessings and grace in my life. My experience of my supply, sufficiency, abundance, blessings and grace is growing and expanding every day in every way."

MY SUPPLY, SUFFICIENCY, ABUNDANCE, BLESSINGS AND GRACE IS GROWING AND EXPANDING EVERY DAY IN EVERY WAY

8. **PLENTY/PROSPERITY** The inner experience of "plenty and prosperity" will follow from alignment with the energy of

"sufficiency and supply". External experiences of plenty and prosperity will increase as you focus on the positive, prosperous thoughts of plenty and abundance and as you increasingly offer thoughts, ideas and attitudes of plenty, prosperity, abundance, supply, sufficiency and blessings to others. What you focus on expands. Plenty and prosperity can manifest in many different ways. The form it takes will depend greatly on your desires, beliefs, expectations, dreams, goals and visions. The more specific you can be about what you want, the greater the likelihood that plenty, prosperity and abundance will manifest in that form. Be open, however, to miraculous and wonderful surprises that will bring you much more joy and fulfillment than you expected, in unexpected ways, or at unexpected times. You always want to be grateful for what you have received if you wish to further increase your prosperity, abundance and plenty. Useful affirmations are: "The divine presence/consciousness within is my source of infinite supply and sufficiency." "Plenty, prosperity, love and blessings come to me, quickly now, under grace, in perfect ways.", or "Everything and everyone prospers and loves me now. I prosper and love everything and everyone now."

PLENTY, PROSPERITY, LOVE AND BLESSINGS
COME TO ME, QUICKLY NOW, UNDER GRACE,
IN PERFECT WAYS

9. **DECREASE/INCREASE** In order to increase gratitude and abundance, plenty and prosperity, decrease negative attitudes, thoughts, judgments and grievances against other people and yourself. Dramatically decrease and then

TO INCREASE GRATITUDE AND ABUNDANCE
DECREASE NEGATIVE ATTITUDES

eliminate your griping and complaining about lack, deprivation, poverty, insufficiency and inadequacy in yourself and others. Let go and release attitudes, phrases and words such as "I can't", "I shouldn't", "It's impossible", and even "I'll try", and "It's difficult". By decreasing negative and limiting thoughts, attitudes, words and feelings, you learn to forgive yourself and others. More miracles come from forgiveness (and gratitude) than anything else. Forgiveness and letting go create a vacuum or space for wonderful, positive, miraculous healing and prosperous circumstances, people, ideas and events to enter your life. It is like clearing your closet of old, worn out clothes; making room for the new, valuable and beautiful. Having decreased the negative and limiting thoughts, feelings and expectations, you can then increase positive, grateful and prosperous thoughts and attitudes. What you focus on expands. What you radiate, you attract. Repeat frequently, for example, a positive affirmation such as, "I love, respect and appreciate the highest, best and most (talented, loving or beautiful) in all people. I now draw to myself the highest, best and most (talented, loving or beautiful) in all people (or clients, customers, friends and colleagues)."

10. **DESERVABILITY/COMMAND** In order to draw experiences of abundance, prosperity and success toward you, become aware of your deservability. You deserve to have good, loving, wonderful, joyful, fulfilling, abundant, prosperous, successful experiences in life. Release negative judgments, beliefs and attitudes of unworthiness or undeservability such as "I don't deserve this"; or "Who am I to deserve this?"; or "He/she deserves this more than I do." Affirm your own value, worth and deservability. Let go of barriers to experiencing this. The divine presence/consciousness, the infinite/creative intelligence dwells within you and equally in

AFFIRM YOUR OWN VALUE, WORTH
AND DESERVABILITY

all others. You can command and affirm your own worth or value. You can command abundance, prosperity, love, health and success by affirming it, by desiring and want it, by believing in and expecting it, and by choosing it. You command it by visualizing and imagining it happening and then by being grateful for attaining it and for the people in your life who helped you attain it. Close your eyes now. Breathe slowly and deeply. Relax. Affirm and command to yourself: "I am worthy of abundance, prosperity, success, health, blessings and love in my life. I feel total sufficiency and infinite supply within me. I deserve it. I ask that divine guidance assist me and guide me. I choose to create abundance and prosperity for myself." Visualize and imagine specific forms of abundance, prosperity, health or love entering your life. Picture the benefits to you. Ask for a higher power to help you. Feel grateful for attaining all the abundance, prosperity, health, blessings and love you desire.

11. **THOUGHTFULNESS/KINDNESS** Being thoughtful to others will generate thoughtfulness from others. What you give is what you receive. What you radiate is what you attract. Being thoughtful, considerate, compassionate and kind benefits others and benefits you. Your abundance,

BEING THOUGHTFUL AND CONSIDERATE
BENEFITS OTHERS AND BENEFITS YOU

prosperity, supply and plenty will grow and expand greatly as you give freely and thoughtfully to others. Positive, loving, prosperous ideas, attitudes and feelings join with these qualities in others. Thoughtfulness and kindness go together. Kind people are loving, caring people to themselves and others. Release resentments, hurts, grievances and anger toward others, and be less defensive and more open to receive. Choose to be less judgmental; choose to be thankful and appreciative of what others have given and what you have received. Choose to rejoice and celebrate in your abundance and in your close, caring relationships.

12. **BLESSINGS/GRACE** When you are thoughtful and kind to yourself and others, when you are thankful and appreciative of what you have received from others, from yourself and from the divine/holy spirit or energy within, your heart will begin to open and you will experience the blessings in your life. Ultimately, you will see that your whole life is a blessing. The more thanks and gratitude you give for the blessings you experience, the more they enter your life. As you

*ULTIMATELY YOU WILL SEE THAT YOUR
WHOLE LIFE IS A BLESSING*

give thanks, as you offer and receive blessings, you will experience grace entering your life. You will begin to experience grace guiding your life, as an unseen force, protecting you, looking over you, nurturing, loving and directing you. The more grace you feel, the more love, joy

*YOU WILL BEGIN TO EXPERIENCE GRACE
GUIDING YOUR LIFE AS AN UNSEEN FORCE,
PROTECTING YOU, LOVING YOU, AND DIRECTING YOU*

and abundance you will experience. Feel gratitude and offer thanks for the blessings in your life. Close your eyes now. Breathe slowly and deeply. Repeat silently to yourself: "I give thanks to the divine/holy spirit or energy (the creative/infinite intelligence) within me for all the blessings and grace in my life. I rejoice in all the love, peace, happiness, joy and abundance that I have received and will increasingly receive and give in my life. Thank you."

Reread the previous twelve steps. Contemplate deeply the significance of these ideas for your life. Do the suggested processes. Then allow yourself to experience the profound, inner transformation taking place.

Though Jeff was only 42, he had extensive arthritis when he attended a weekend seminar a few years ago. He wrote us a beautiful letter following the seminar, which talks about the healing process and how giving and receiving love are one. Here are some excerpts:

Dear Phil and Teresa,

Meeting you brought a lot of joy. Thank you very much for your love, kindness and generosity. The work you are doing is very important and the love that it gives and receives is a function of the love you give and receive. . . .My own healing process has been lengthy. . . .I attended the seminar to share, or should I say to be a vehicle for the manifestation of love. I received reaffirmation that my healing was complete and I was a very healthy person.

Fear ◗ Love ◗ Oneness. Rejoice my brother and sister. The universe celebrates. The candles on the cake were almost burnt all the way down while waiting for me. My love to you both."

Karen was moderately anxious and depressed when she attended our weekend seminar in early 1985. Thirty-eight, divorced, unemployed with two children, she was confused about the direction of her life. Her self-esteem was tenuous. She was, however, a deeply spiritual person and I found her warm, likable and easy to relate to. Karen's experience at the seminar was extremely uplifting. She had the special gift for communicating in words the feelings she had for other people. She is perhaps one of the best examples I know of the statement, "You receive what you give and you attract what you radiate." I have always been deeply touched by her presence and the moving letters she has written me and my wife.

Dear Phil,

I just wanted to say thank you again for all of your help, supportiveness and caring during the weekend seminar. I gained so much from the experience. Every day I thank God for the opportunity to bring so much healing and happiness into my life. The good feelings are continuing for me. This has been a beautiful time - no depression or anxiety, just feelings of peace and serenity. I wish I could better express the feelings in my heart but just know that I appreciate your efforts and pray for you always. I'm so glad that giving and receiving are one because that means you'll receive all the happiness and love you've given!

With gratitude,

Karen

Karen offered to be one of my assistants at the next weekend seminar. Five months later, after assisting at another weekend seminar, Karen writes:

Thanks again for the opportunity to assist at the last seminar. The experience was as usual very fulfilling and meaningful to me. At the risk of repeating myself, I am always deeply touched by the beauty and courage of the attendees, by you, and even myself. You truly are a minister of God - and a very inspiring one. Thank you for creating such a wonderful, warm, safe, loving, sharing, blessed (and fun) experience for people. This work is so important. I know you are blessed a million times for doing it. And I feel blessed to be a little part of it. Thank you.

Peace and Love,

Finally, Karen writes again some months later.

Infinite thanks for giving me the opportunity to assist again at the seminar weekend. (Karen, by this time, had taken several of our advanced level courses and seminars.) It was a deeply moving experience and I feel so lucky and blessed to have been part of all the healing that happened. You bring so much love into the lives of everyone who comes to you for help and you have touched mine in a very profound way. Thank you for all the joy and beauty and peace and playfulness you've brought into my life. I am very grateful.

Needless to say, Karen's expression of gratitude and thankfulness is deeply appreciated and touching. Not long after writing this letter, Karen found a successful, full-time job in the business world where she is of great service to others. Her abundance blossomed in all areas due to her great faith and compassion. We will always cherish the light, love and blessings that she brought into our lives and the lives of the many people she assisted at our seminars. She, like each of us, is a precious gift to humanity.

GRATITUDE/ABUNDANCE HOME WORK/PLAY SHEET

A. LIST TEN PEOPLE OR SITUATIONS FOR WHICH YOU ARE MOST THANKFUL, APPRECIATIVE AND GRATEFUL AND WHAT IT IS FOR WHICH YOU ARE THANKFUL AND GRATEFUL.

1.

2.

3.

4.

5.

6.

7.

8.

9.

10.

B. WHAT YOU FOCUS ON EXPANDS. WHAT YOU RADIATE, YOU AT-TRACT. CONTEMPLATE EVERYTHING YOU HAVE TO BE GRATEFUL FOR TODAY AND THEN SHARE YOUR EXPERIENCE OF GRATITUDE AND APPRECIATION WITH AS MANY PEOPLE AS POSSIBLE FOR ONE MONTH. EACH WEEK WRITE DOWN YOUR EXPERIENCE AT THE END OF THE WEEK.

C. LIST FIVE THINGS YOU HAVE AND CAN FREELY GIVE TO OTHERS IN YOUR LIFE, OR FIVE WAYS YOU FEEL ABUNDANT AND ARE WILL-ING TO GIVE FREELY TO OTHERS. THEN REFLECT ON HOW YOU CAN EXPAND THEM.

1.

2.

3.

4.

5.

D. CELEBRATE AND REJOICE AT WHAT YOU HAVE GIVEN AND RECEIVED. CHOOSE TO BE GRATEFUL IN ADVANCE FOR ALL THE POSITIVE EXPERIENCES AND PEOPLE YOU WILL SOON ENCOUNTER. ASK THE CREATIVE/INFINITE INTELLIGENCE, THE DIVINE/HOLY SPIRIT OR ENERGY WITHIN TO HELP YOU.

E. CLOSE YOUR EYES. RELAX. BREATHE DEEPLY. ASK THE CREATIVE/INFINITE INTELLIGENCE, THE DIVINE/HOLY SPIRIT OR ENERGY TO HELP YOU CONTACT THE DIVINE, INFINITE PRESENCE OR CONSCIOUSNESS WITHIN YOU.

ONE MONTH PROGRAM FOR INCREASING AND ENHANCING GRATITUDE AND ABUNDANCE

F. REPEAT THE FOLLOWING AFFIRMATIONS TO YOURSELF 10-20 TIMES OR MORE PER DAY FOR THE FIRST WEEK:
    1. I REJOICE AND GIVE THANKS FOR THE EVERFLOWING, ALWAYS ABUNDANT SOURCE OF INFINITE SUPPLY, SUFFICIENCY, BLESSINGS AND GRACE IN MY LIFE.
    2. MY EXPERIENCE OF MY INNER SUPPLY, SUFFICIENCY, ABUNDANCE, BLESSINGS AND GRACE IS FLOWING AND EXPANDING EVERY DAY IN EVERY WAY.

G. REPEAT THE FOLLOWING AFFIRMATIONS TO YOURSELF 10-20 TIMES OR MORE PER DAY FOR THE SECOND WEEK:
    1. THE DIVINE PRESENCE/CONSCIOUSNESS WITHIN IS MY SOURCE OF INFINITE SUPPLY, SUFFICIENCY, ABUNDANCE, BLESSINGS AND GRACE.
    2. PLENTY, PROSPERITY, ABUNDANCE AND BLESSINGS COME TO ME NOW, QUICKLY, UNDER GRACE AND IN PERFECT WAYS.
    3. EVERYTHING AND EVERYONE PROSPERS (OR LOVES) ME NOW. I PROSPER (OR LOVE) EVERYTHING AND EVERYONE NOW.

H. REPEAT THE FOLLOWING AFFIRMATIONS TO YOURSELF 10-20 TIMES PER DAY OR MORE FOR THE THIRD WEEK:
    1.   I LOVE, RESPECT AND APPRECIATE THE HIGHEST, BEST AND MOST (TALENTED, LOVING, WISEST OR BEAUTIFUL) IN ALL PEOPLE (OR ALL CLIENTS, CUSTOMERS, FRIENDS, FAMILY AND COLLEAGUES).
    2.   I AM WORTHY OF ABUNDANCE, PROSPERITY, SUCCESS, HEALTH AND LOVE IN MY LIFE. I THANK YOU. I FEEL TOTAL SUFFICIENCY AND INFINITE SUPPLY, BLESSINGS AND GRACE WITHIN ME. I DESERVE IT.

I. REPEAT THE FOLLOWING AFFIRMATIONS TO YOURSELF 10-20 TIMES PER DAY OR MORE FOR THE FOURTH WEEK:
    1.   I GIVE THANKS TO THE DIVINE/HOLY SPIRIT OR ENERGY (THE CREATIVE/INFINITE INTELLIGENCE) WITHIN ME FOR ALL THE SUFFICIENCY, SUPPLY, ABUNDANCE, BLESSINGS AND GRACE IN MY LIFE.
    2.   I REJOICE IN ALL THE GOOD, LOVING, JOYFUL ABUNDANCE AND ALL THE BLESSINGS AND GRACE THAT I HAVE RECEIVED AND WILL INCREASINGLY RECEIVE AND GIVE IN MY LIFE. THANK YOU!

NOTES:

CHAPTER TWELVE

CONTACTING A UNIVERSAL SOURCE OR CENTER WITHIN

The following guidelines for contacting a universal Source or Center dwelling within yourself are perhaps the most important of the twelve Principles of Well-Being.

1. **GRATITUDE/ABUNDANCE** You can learn to experience more gratitude and abundance by contacting the infinite Source or Center of fulfillment within you. Gratitude is a powerful inner experience for bringing miracles to you. Learn to be grateful by being thankful and appreciative of all the experiences, people and events in your life. Then you will feel like rejoicing and celebrating as an inner joyfulness arises from the center of your Self/Being. To experience more gratitude, choose to be defenseless and receptive to wonderful, loving and prosperous experiences and begin to experience a divine presence or consciousness coming from within. This presence will guide you to greater experiences of love, peace, joy, sufficiency and supply. Align yourself with this energy by increasing your awareness and by turning within for guidance. Releasing negative attitudes, thoughts

and judgments, being more forgiving, thoughtful, kind, loving and compassionate will help a great deal. Realize that you deserve to contact the all-fulfilling, consciousness of love, gratitude and abundance. When you do, you will experience blessings and grace entering your life.

YOU WILL EXPERIENCE GRACE AND BLESSINGS
ENTERING YOUR LIFE

2. **SOURCE/CENTER** A universal Source or Center is the place within you where deep love, peace, joy, fulfillment, creativity, gratitude, abundance, blessings, holiness and grace can be found. It is also the source of your inner strength, intuition, determination, compassion and resourcefulness. Sometimes the Source/Center is referred to as the inner Guide, Teacher, Master, Christ, Buddha, Jehovah, Guru or Voice. The creative/infinite intelligence (divine/

THE SOURCE/CENTER IS SOMETIMES CALLED
THE INNER GUIDE OR THE INNER TEACHER,
MASTER, CHRIST, BUDDHA, JEHOVA,
GURU OR VOICE

holy spirit or energy) can help you contact this Center. An attitude of willingness or receptivity is necessary. Be open to receiving whatever experiences your inner Self has to offer you. Quiet your restless "ego" mind. The agitated, tense, hurt, angry, frustrated, or guilty part of you (the "ego") always experiences itself as separate from the true Source or Center of your Being. It experiences darkness and limitation, whereas your Source/Center experiences light and expansion. The "ego" experiences fear, conflict and depression, while your Source/Center experiences love, peace and joy.

3. **ENVIRONMENT/SANCTUARY** To contact the Source or Center, create a comfortable, relaxed, pleasant and safe environment free of fear, anxiety, disturbance and distraction.

It can be in a group setting, such as a meditation center, church, synagogue, or spiritual retreat that is especially

CREATE A COMFORTABLE, RELAXED, PLEASANT AND SAFE ENVIRONMENT

designed to facilitate the inward turning. The additional benefit of being in this environment is the positive group support and energy available. It serves as a kind of sanctuary away from the hustle and bustle of the world. But you can create a peaceful, quiet, meditative environment within your home or office as well. At first, it is preferable to use the same safe, comfortable environment each time you practice contacting the universal Source/Center within you. Next, create an inner environment or sanctuary within you that is safe, peaceful, beautiful and loving. Close your eyes. Relax.

NEXT CREATE AN INNER ENVIRONMENT OR SANCTUARY WITHIN YOU

Take a few slow, deep breaths. Visualize a place that is safe, peaceful, beautiful and relaxing. Allow yourself to experience the sounds, sights and smells of this inner sanctuary.

4. **SING/CHANT** You may discover that accessing the universal Source/Center is easier at first by singing or chanting some phrases, prayer, mantra or affirmation out loud, either by yourself or with a group. When you are alone, it is often beneficial to listen to soothing music, a song, prayer, or a mantra for 5-15 minutes before turning your attention inward. Classical music, Gregorian or Sanskrit chants, Christian, Jewish or Buddhist prayers or songs, and new age music can be helpful and uplifting. As you listen, sing or chant with the music, allow your mind to focus inward beyond the concerns, worries, aspirations and upsets of the day. If you have selected the music, song, prayer or mantra carefully, you will

find yourself being drawn inward toward an altered state of consciousness. Allow yourself to yield to the rhythm and

> *FIND YOURSELF BEING DRAWN INTO*
> *AN ALTERED STATE OF CONSCIOUSNESS*

tempo of the music. Begin to breathe slowly and deeply. While you are doing this, make sure you are sitting in a comfortable, relaxed posture. It is preferable to keep your arms and legs uncrossed so the energy can flow easily and naturally.

5. **CALM/RELAX** Although it is helpful to listen, sing or chant along with the music at first, you can also just close your eyes and begin to calm your agitated "ego" mind by focusing on the breath. (You could also do this after listening to your music.) Allow the breath to rise and fall naturally. Repeat the words "calm" on the in-breath and "relax" on the out-breath, or "peace" on the in-breath and "love" on the out-breath to help quiet your mind. You can also use other phrases, prayers or mantras, such as "Christ and Mary", "Jehovah and Yahweh", "Buddha and Being", or "Om Namah Shivaya" as you focus on the breath. You may find that holding your breath for a count of three between the in-breath and out-breath will help you become still and quiet more easily. As you continue to repeat your chosen phase, be aware that the breath is the mediator between the mind and body and is the gateway to the universal Source/Center. As you hold your breath for a count of

> *THE BREATH IS THE MEDIATOR BETWEEN*
> *THE MIND AND THE BODY, AND IS THE GATEWAY*
> *TO THE UNIVERSAL SOURCE/CENTER*

three, focus your awareness on the space or pause between the breath. Allow yourself to enter into an altered state of consciousness. You may find that visualizing yourself slowly descending ten flights by elevator or escalator will deepen the experience of calm and relaxation.

6. **WITNESS/OBSERVE** While you are breathing in and out, slowly and deeply, repeating your chosen words, allow yourself to witness your thoughts, feelings, sensations and experiences as they come into your awareness. Just observe

WITNESS YOUR THOUGHTS, FEELINGS, SENSATIONS AND EXPERIENCES

them as if you were a photographer looking through the lens of a camera. Be a curious, interested observer without allowing yourself to be attached to these experiences. Don't judge, analyze or compare them to anyone else's experience. Just accept the feelings, thoughts and sensations as yours. Imagine they are clouds floating in the sky, or logs floating down a river. Observe them. Witness them. Let them float by. Then bring your awareness back to your breath and your chosen phrase. This centering technique will gradually help you still and quiet your "ego" mind as you begin to contact the universal Source/Center. As you become proficient at this exercise, you will discover that the "Witness" or "Observer" is the same as the Source/Center within you and also the place where you can begin to access deeper wisdom and intuition.

7. **TEACHER/VOICE** As you practice breathing, slowly and gradually, while repeating your phrase, you will find yourself entering into a deeper and deeper state of calm, relaxation, peace and love. Your mind and emotions will quiet. Eventually, you will begin to contact the universal Source within. This process is easy, effortless, natural and simple. It is, however, important to be patient with yourself and to persist over time with the centering practice. You will discover an inner teacher having great knowledge which exists within you. It is a quiet, gentle inner voice that can guide you and

AN INNER TEACHER OR VOICE WITH GREAT
KNOWLEDGE EXISTS WITHIN YOU

answer your concerns and questions from a profound, wise place within you. An attitude of willingness and receptivity are necessary. Frequently, answers to your concerns will just bubble up while you are deeply relaxed, centered or meditating in this way. Some people find it additionally helpful to visualize themselves surrounded by a white light. Others find it beneficial to picture themselves walking from their inner sanctuary through a forest and field to a one-room schoolhouse. Here they find a wise, loving and compassionate teacher who may also be surrounded by a radiant and loving light.

8. **ASK/LISTEN** The inner Teacher or Voice will be available to you when your "ego" mind has become still and quiet. At that point, reflect carefully on the question or questions you want to ask. They should be clear, specific, brief, and asked one at a time. Release all judgments, investments and attachments to the answer (what you want to hear, feel or see). Allow your inner Teacher to speak to you. Open your heart

ALLOW YOUR INNER TEACHER TO SPEAK TO YOU
OPEN YOUR HEART AND MIND
BE A RECEPTIVE CHANNEL

and mind to being a receptive channel for the information. Be patient with yourself and with your Teacher/Voice. Listen for quiet, gentle words. You may see an image or symbol. Pay close attention to your feelings, sensations and emotional sense. You may experience a shift of energy in some part of your body. Whatever you experience is perfect for you at that moment. Do not prejudge or pre-select the kind or form of the experience. Allow your inner Teacher/Voice to guide you to what you need to know, hear or see. Allow a deeper intuition or wisdom to arise from within.

9. **EXPECT/ACCEPT** Although it is important not to prejudge the answer, it is equally important to expect an answer. If you don't receive a response immediately, be kind to yourself and

> *IT IS EQUALLY IMPORTANT TO*
> *EXPECT AN ANSWER*

patient with your inner knower or guide. Relax some more. Keep breathing slowly and deeply. Keep listening. The process is simple, natural, effortless. You may need to still and quiet your "ego" mind even further. It is in the inner silence that the inner Guide/Knower will speak to you. Once you have received the answer to your question, permit yourself to accept it. It may or may not be what you consciously expected to hear, or it may not be information that you ordinarily would have access to with your "ego" mind. In fact, since the information is coming from your higher Source or Center, the guidance will frequently come from a deeper, more intuitive place. No matter what the response, accept it for now and choose to be at peace. Love yourself. If the guidance is truly from your inner Teacher, you will naturally experience a greater harmony and alignment with yourself, others and the universe. If you receive nothing new, choose to be at peace and love yourself.

10. **SEND/TRANSMIT** If you receive guidance, accept it. If you do not, perhaps you are not supposed to receive information at the moment. Quiet your mind and listen further or listen again another day. Patience and persistence are important. Take the opportunity to send healing messages of love and peace to other people. With your eyes still closed and while

> *SEND HEALING MESSAGES OF LOVE AND PEACE*
> *TO OTHER PEOPLE*

you are breathing slowly and deeply, visualize yourself trans-
mitting healing energy (love, peace, joy, forgiveness, compassion) to people in your life. Since all minds are already joined
at the level of the Self/Being, the healing energy you send will
be simultaneously received. Ask that the creative/infinite intelligence help you with this process. You can also send the

ALL MINDS ARE ALREADY JOINED
AT THE LEVEL OF SELF/BEING
ASK THE CREATIVE/INFINITE INTELLIGENCE
TO HELP YOU

healing energy of love to a city, state, region or the planet
Earth. You can transmit healing energy by visualizing, sensing or feeling yourself in a state of "oneness". Visualize yourself and the other person or place surrounded and joined by
a loving, healing light. Naturally, while you send and transmit healing love, peace, joy and "oneness", you will receive it
simultaneously.

11. **RECORD/REPEAT** You will often learn more from your experience if you record your answers, responses or guidance
in some way. Some people find it valuable to surround the

RECORD YOUR ANSWERS OR GUIDANCE

recording instrument with white light. If you have a record,
you will find it easier to follow your progress over time. In
this way you can also check on the value of the information
received in the days, weeks or months ahead. It isn't necessary to record the information to benefit from the medita-
tion/centering process; however, it can be useful. The
information you receive will often give you specific advice on
what to do, where to go, with whom to interact, and what to
say. Sometimes it will just clarify the way things are. If the
information does not bring you more peace, love, joy, har-

mony or forgiveness, it may be coming from your "ego" and not your inner Source/Center. Then it would not be wise for you to act on the answer without listening again, with a more peaceful mind, for the quiet answer. Repeat the sequence of steps described here frequently. You may want to repeat them the same day, the next day, or every day. It is very important for you to be patient and compassionate with yourself. Be persistent and love yourself. Be at peace and in harmony with your magnificence.

12. **PURPOSE/VISION** You can use the meditation/centering process to answer questions, to relax and calm yourself, and to deepen your connection with your universal Source. One of the most valuable ways to utilize the meditation process is to discover your highest purpose and vision in life. Purpose and vision is the first of the twelve Principles of Well-Being,

USE THE MEDITATION PROCESS TO DISCOVER YOUR PURPOSE/VISION IN LIFE

and the first essential ingredient for high well-being and mental health. You can ask the inner Source/Teacher to guide you to a clearer sense of meaning, direction and purpose and to a clearer sense of your true Identity. By using this process of meditation/centering, you will discover how you can use your talents, abilities, skills and unique personality qualities to serve yourself, your family, and others in the highest possible way. Discover that at the core of your Self/Being, your Source/Center, is radiant light and love, and your ultimate purpose and vision is to be a channel or instrument for that light and love. You will, at the very least, discover your own magnificence, greatness and uniqueness.

THE CORE OF YOUR SELF/BEING IS RADIANT LIGHT

YOUR ULTIMATE PURPOSE AND VISION IS TO BE A CHANNEL OF LIGHT AND LOVE

Read and reread the previous twelve steps. Practice the meditation/centering process as often as possible, preferably once or twice a day. Be patient and yet persistent. Allow this natural, simple and effortless process help you contact your universal Source/Center. Allow yourself to receive answers and guidance from your inner Teacher, your inner Voice. Allow yourself to experience the profound inner transformation that will take place.

When Marsha came to see me, she was in her early 30's, married with no children. She was distressed over conflicts at work and also at home with her husband Bill. Marsha had a very responsible position in a well-know legal institution but felt constantly under pressure and criticism from a male co-worker. She also felt neglected by her husband who appeared to be more interested in his career, tennis, and his male friends than in her. It was obvious that she needed to relax more, increase her self-esteem, express and assert herself more, and learn how to contact her creative, infinite/intelligence or inner teacher.

The meditative/relaxation exercise was very helpful to her. Without much difficulty, she was able to contact an inner teacher or wisdom figure who resembled a yoga teacher she had met years earlier and liked very much. She felt surrounded and protected by the radiant white light in the meditation/relaxation exercise and received inner messages that both reassured her and guided her. The inner messages conveyed to her that she was loved, that she needed to choose and practice peace and forgiveness more, that she would benefit from looking on the positive side of situations, and that everything would work out for her. During the therapy sessions, Marsha also learned to stop belittling herself by "shoulding" on herself and learned to focus on her positive qualities, talents and abilities more.

I helped Marsha clarify her career, relationship and personal goals. As she became more relaxed, more self-confident, and more in tune with her inner guidance, she was able to more often speak up at work and at home. She spoke to her boss and requested and received a transfer to another department. Marsha invited Bill to some of her therapy sessions. These sessions led to more effective communication (listening, expressing and problem-solving), and increased the sharing of affection between them.

Eventually, Marsha and Bill attended my weekend seminar on well-being and experienced a further enrichment and uplift in their relationship. Marsha was then able to help and support Bill through a stressful time in his job during a corporate "shake-up". This brought them even closer together. When we terminated therapy, Marsha was much happier at work (she'd received a substantial bonus as well), at home and, most importantly, with herself. She called one year later to say things were still going well and she was very thankful for what she had learned in the therapy sessions and at the seminar. She reported that she continued to meditate on a regular basis and found it extremely valuable.

Bill called me two years later to say that Marsha had just given birth to a baby boy and was ecstatic. Moreover, six months earlier, he had transferred to a new job, was managing a store, and was very happy. Both Bill and Marsha told me that they regularly listened to my audio tapes on "Creating and Manifesting What You Want" and "The Inner Journey to the Higher Self/Being", and found them extremely helpful. Marsha, in particular, was in continuous contact with her inner guide/teacher.

THE INNER JOURNEY TO THE HIGHER SELF/BEING

Follow the instructions for the Meditative/Relaxation Journey to the Inner Sanctuary in Chapter Two. Then proceed on the inner journey to the higher Self/Being.

At one end of the inner sanctuary, you will find a path. Get on the path and follow it. Soon you will pass under a gate with a sign above it that says "Enter". You continue following the path to a forest. It is very dark in the forest. It is difficult to follow the path because of the darkness. Nevertheless, you do follow it as it winds its way through the darkness of the forest. You may be able to hear the rustling of leaves on the trees, or animals scurrying about, or the wind blowing through the trees. You may smell the fragrance of the forest as you follow the path. It is very dark in the forest but ahead of you, perhaps 50 feet, you see a glimmer of light at the end of the forest. You walk toward the light and as you get closer, it becomes brighter and clearer.

As you approach the light, you notice that the path enters a field. You walk toward the field and see, in front of you, a bubbling brook. As you walk on the path along the brook, you notice that the brook is clogged with logs, leaves and debris, and the water is not flowing very freely. You continue on the path next to the brook a little way until you come to a bridge across it. Get on the bridge (which represents the creative/infinite intelligence, the divine holy spirit or energy within you), and take it across the brook. You continue to follow the path through the field and then you see, about 100 feet ahead of you, a large fire burning it a pit. You walk on the path toward the fire. As you approach the blazing fire that roars five to six feet high, you offer all your anger, hurt, fear, grief, guilt, shame, negatives, judgments, demands, attach thoughts, illnesses, diseases and pain to the fire. You actually dump, release and let go of all your emotional upset, distress, and negative thoughts, ideas and beliefs into the fire. As you do so, the fire consumes them.

You continue to follow the path past the fire. Up ahead of you, perhaps another 100 feet, you see a one room schoolhouse. You walk on the path toward it. In front of the one room schoolhouse are three steps. You walk toward the steps. You climb the three steps of the schoolhouse. You notice the door is open and you enter. Ahead of you are five rows of chairs. In the front row is a blackboard and desk. You walk to the front of the schoolhouse and sit down in the first seat of the first row. As you look up, you see standing in front of you next to the desk, a very wise and very loving teacher. This wise and loving teacher (who represents your higher Self or Being) is so compassionate, so understanding, so wise, and so loving. You look into the eyes of this wise and loving teacher, and you feel safe, secure and comforted.

Just then your wise and loving teacher raises his/her hands to his/her sides. As you look into the hands of your wise and loving teacher, you see two spheres of radiant and loving light coming out of them. These spheres of light are so radiant and so loving. They enter directly into your heart. As they enter your heart, there is an explosion of light and love and you begin to feel the light flowing through your heart to the top of your head and the tips of your toes. You can feel a continuous stream of loving light flowing through you and entering into every artery, vein, muscle, tissue and cell of your body. Open your heart and mind. The light is the light of love. It is so soft, so gentle, so compassionate, so strong and so healing. You can see, feel, touch and sense the light as it flows through your entire body and mind. The light is so caring, so kind, so understanding, so wise, so forgiving and so loving. You begin to notice the light encircling your whole being. It envelopes you in love. As you look toward your wise and loving teacher, you notice that he or she is now enveloped in the loving and radiant light. As you notice the light around your teacher, the lights begin to join. As they do, the light becomes infinitely more powerful, more loving and more healing. Now the lights have joined and become one.

You then look again into your teacher's eyes. They are so wise and loving and compassionate. You begin to formulate a question in your mind that you would like to ask your inner teacher or guide. Contemplate for several seconds the question you would like to ask and get clear about it in your mind. Now ask your question of your wise and loving teacher and be open to receive the answer in whatever form it comes. The answer may come verbally or non-verbally, symbolically, as an image, feeling, sensation or thought. Just be open to receiving it in whatever form it comes. Open your heart and mind. Take several seconds to receive it. Perhaps you would like to ask a second question. Take 15-30 seconds to formulate this second question and again be open to receiving the answer in whatever form it comes. Once again, open your mind and open your heart. Now your wise and loving teacher has a gift or message for you. It may be something you've been waiting to receive or hear for a long, long time; perhaps your entire life. Be open to receiving this gift or message in whatever form it comes; verbal, material, symbolic, a feeling, a sensation, an image, etc.

Now say goodbye to your wise and loving teacher in whatever way seems comfortable and appropriate to you. Thank him or her for whatever answers, gifts or messages you have received. Walk toward the door of the one room schoolhouse. The teacher, representing your inner or higher Self or Being, will always be there waiting for you. For now though, follow the path back across the field. As you do so, you see the ashes of the burning fire that has consumed your anger, hurt, fear, guilt and negatives. If there are any remaining upsets, dump them in the burning ashes now. Then continue on the path toward the bubbling brook. As you approach the brook, you see the bridge. You walk on the bridge that crosses the brook and as you do, you notice that the brook is flowing easily, smoothly and naturally now. The brook is very pure and crystal clean and murmurs softly and sweetly. (The bridge represents the creative/infinite intelligence, the divine/holy spirit or energy within you.)

You follow the path to the forest. Although the forest is still dark, the path is very clear now because you are surrounded by a radiant light that emblazons it. The dark forest becomes illuminated from the path with the light radiant within you and around you. The entire forest seems to be lit up by this radiant and glowing light. As you walk on the path to your inner sanctuary, you pass through the gate once again. As you look up, you see a sign above the gate that says, "Remember the Light Within" and "Remember to See the Light Within Others". You then continue to walk on the path to your inner sanctuary, your place of safety, peace, beauty, well-being and love.

Sit or lie down in the inner sanctuary for a few moments. Allow yourself to once more enjoy the sounds, sights and smells of the inner sanctuary and the sense of deep peace, contentment and well-being. In just a few moments you are going to walk over to the elevator. The elevator will then return from the first floor to the tenth floor. When you get to the tenth floor, your eyes will be open. You'll feel refreshed, alert, peaceful, renewed, and with your consciousness back in the room. Walk over to the elevator now. Get on the first floor. 1....2....3....4....5.....6....7....8....9....10 The elevator opens on the tenth floor. Your eyes are open. You are refreshed, alert, peaceful and renewed, and your consciousness is back in the room.

UNIVERSAL SOURCE/CENTER
HOME WORK/PLAY SHEET

A. LIST FIVE UPSETTING OR DISTRESSING EMOTIONS THAT MOST OFTEN CHARACTERIZE YOUR "EGO" STATE OF CONSCIOUSNESS; SUCH AS FEAR, ANGER, HURT, FRUSTRATION, GUILT, ETC.:

   1.

   2.

   3.

   4.

THEN LIST UP TO FIVE UPLIFTING EMOTIONS THAT YOU WOULD LIKE TO EXPERIENCE WHEN YOU MAKE CONTACT WITH YOUR UNIVERSAL CENTER/SOURCE OR SELF/BEING; SUCH AS LOVE, PEACE, JOY, HAPPINESS, ECSTASY:

   1.

   2.

   3.

   4.

   5.

B. LIST THREE QUESTIONS YOU WOULD LIKE ANSWERED BY A WISE, LOVING INNER TEACHER, GUIDE OR VOICE; OR LIST THREE PROBLEMS TO WHICH YOU WOULD LIKE SOLUTIONS:

   1.

   2.

   3.

C. LIST THE NAMES OF FIVE PEOPLE OR PLACES TO WHOM YOU WOULD LIKE TO SEND HEALING MESSAGES OF LOVE AND PEACE:

   1.

   2.

   3.

   4.

   5.

D. WRITE DOWN ANY INFORMATION, IDEAS, SYMBOLS, IMAGES, PERCEPTIONS, MESSAGES, HUNCHES, FEELINGS, SENSATIONS OR GUIDANCE YOU RECEIVE FROM YOUR INNER TEACHER, GUIDE, VOICE OR SELF/BEING (AFTER YOU HAVE COMPLETED THE MEDITATIVE/RELAXATION PROCESS):

_____

_____

_____

_____

_____

_____

E. LIST THREE GOALS YOU WOULD LIKE TO ACCOMPLISH IN THE NEAR FUTURE (3-4 MONTHS); NEXT YEAR; AND IN YOUR LIFE:

NEAR FUTURE	ONE YEAR	LIFE
1.	1.	1.
2.	2.	2.
3.	3.	3.

THEN WRITE DOWN YOUR HIGHEST PURPOSE AND VISION IN LIFE AND BRIEFLY STATE HOW THESE GOALS ARE ALIGNED WITH THEM:

_____

_____

_____

_____

_____

_____

_____

_____

FINALLY, HOW IS YOUR HIGHEST PURPOSE AND VISION IN LIFE RELATED TO YOUR UNDERSTANDING OF YOUR HIGHER SELF/BEING?

_____

_____

_____

_____

_____

_____

YOU CAN USE THE "INNER JOURNEY TO THE SELF/BEING" AND THE "INNER JOURNEY FROM DIVINE LOVE: THE ADVANCED FORM OF THE CREATION AND MANIFESTATION PROCESS" TO HELP YOU ANSWER THESE QUESTIONS.

INNER JOURNEY FROM DIVINE LOVE: THE ADVANCED FORM OF THE CREATION AND MANIFESTATION PROCESS

1. **MEDITATION/CONTEMPLATION** Close your eyes, relax and meditate on your purpose and vision in life and on what goals you might pursue. Contemplate the significance of these goals and your purpose and vision in life.

2. **SELF/BEING** Continue to meditate and contemplate until you experience some inner movement from within your Self/Being. Allow goals to bubble up from within the stillness of your Self/Being.

3. **HIGHEST GOOD/INFINITE INTELLIGENCE** Ask that the goals bubbling up from your Self/Being be for your highest good and the highest good of all people involved. Ask the creative/infinite intelligence (divine/holy spirit or energy) to help you to do this.

4. **FAITH/TRUST** Ask for faith that the goal(s) you are pursuing are aligned with your highest Self/Being. Trust in the creative/infinite intelligence, divine/holy spirit or energy to guide you toward your highest purpose and vision in life.

5. **SURRENDER/LOVE** Surrender your personal "ego" will to the divine will. Ask that not your "ego's" will, but the Self/Being's will be done. Allow yourself to feel love in your heart and ask that all goals come from love and be in the service of love.

6. **PURPOSE/VISION** Remind yourself that your highest purpose and vision in life is divine love. Ask that the divine/holy spirit or energy align all your goals with divine love and with your Self/Being.

7. **WANTS/GOALS** Clarify your wants and goals reflecting on how they serve divine love and the core of your Self/Being. Write down these wants and goals as soon as you can.

8. **CHOICES/DECISIONS** Consciously choose to create the attainment of these wants and goals. Decide to actively pursue them as long as they are aligned with your Self/Being and Divine Love.

9. **COMMITMENT/PERSISTENCE** Commit yourself to attaining these goals. Take the appropriate actions and persist until the goals are attained or you receive inner guidance to change the goals.

10. **ACTIONS/PLANS** Engage in actions designed to move you toward your goals. Realize that each goal requires a series of sub-goals or steps on the journey to completion. Listen within to make sure your actions are aligned with the divine plan of the Self/Being and not the "ego's" plan.

11. **CREATE/ADAPT** Create steps and sub-goals, take actions and receive inner and outer feedback and guidance. Then adapt and adjust your steps and actions. Then create again, act again and make further adaptations and adjustments until you attain your goal(s).

12. **GRATITUDE/BLESSINGS** Ask the divine/holy spirit or energy, the creative/infinite intelligence to help you to feel grateful for whatever you attain. Relinquish all attachment to the benefits or results of your actions. Allow yourself to feel blessed that all your actions and the results of your actions are instruments of divine love and are aligned with your higher Self/Being.

NOTES:

EPILOGUE

From the vantage point of Self/Being, the Kingdom of Heaven is always going on in this very instant. We always have a choice

THE KINGDOM OF HEAVEN IS ALWAYS GOING ON IN THIS VERY INSTANT

between the reactive level of the ego which generates fear, hurt, anger, guilt and suffering, or the level of Self/Being, of divine Reality, which generates love, peace, joy, gratitude, abundance and grace. When we yield to the Self/Being, when we turn within to the creative/infinite intelligence (the divine/holy spirit or energy) for guidance, we learn to experience the Kingdom of Heaven here and now. The great Masters always say, "I am with you always", and "I am love". If we center ourselves, if we go within to

"I AM WITH YOU ALWAYS AND I AM LOVE"

the core of our Self/Being, we discover that the Kingdom of Heaven is within us always in the form of love. As we align ourselves with that force of love, our life takes on a new coloration, our level of well-being jumps to a new level and our capacity to serve our fellow human beings coming from a place of love greatly expands. Let us ask then that all barriers to love's presence be removed. Let us open our hearts and be grateful for being alive and for being our unique selves. Let us be grateful for what we have received and for what we have to give. For it is in giving love that we receive it, and it is in opening our hearts that we experience the divine presence of love which protects and guides us.

IT IS IN GIVING LOVE THAT WE RECEIVE IT
IT IS IN OPENING OUR HEARTS THAT
WE EXPERIENCE THE DIVINE PRESENCE
OF LOVE WHICH PROTECTS
AND GUIDES US

SUMMARY OF THE TWELVE PRINCIPLES OF WELL-BEING

You can transform the quality of your well-being, your mental health, and your life.

1. **PURPOSE/VISION** Creating and developing a sense of purpose and vision in life is the first essential ingredient for a high state of well-being and mental health. It is as if you were the captain of a ship and had to create a destination that would chart the course of your entire life. You would need to have a vision of who you were and where you wanted to go before planning the journey. A clearly defined sense of purpose, like a long-range goal, serves that function. By clarifying your purpose and vision in life in alignment with your true Self/Being, you can and will initiate a powerful and exciting process leading to an enriching and uplifting lifelong goal.

2. **CREATION/MANIFESTATION** You can learn how to be a creator rather than a reactor to the circumstances of your life. Learn to clarify what you want and to align your goals with your larger purpose and vision in life. Then consciously choose to create and manifest your goals, visualize them being attained and experience the benefits of attaining your goals in advance. Feel grateful to other people for helping you and ask that the goal be for your highest good. Ask that a higher power (creative/infinite intelligence) assist you in attaining your goal. Surrender the goal to this higher power and connect with that part of you that experiences love. Then allow that love to flow through you and connect with the creative/infinite intelligence.

3. **ATTITUDES/THOUGHTS** Mental attitudes and thoughts generate energy. This energy becomes projected by the

mind onto the screen of the world and is then reflected back to you, like a mirror, in the attitudes, feelings and behavior of other people as they interact with you. Since your mind is like a magnet, it will also draw to you positive or negative events, circumstances and people, depending on whether you hold positive or negative mental attitudes, thoughts and beliefs. If you are attuned to higher consciousness, your positive, optimistic and forgiving attitudes, thoughts and energy will resonate with and be amplified by the positive energy of others.

4. **RE-PERCEIVE/REFRAME** You can learn to re-perceive and reframe situations, events and people in a more positive, constructive and uplifting way. What you previously perceived through a dark lens or frame can be seen, with the help of creative/infinite intelligence, through a light lens. You can learn to look for the lessons inherent in every situation and in the process change unpleasant, unfortunate appearing experiences into healing, positive ones. In this way, you can discover great wisdom and profound teachings in all your experiences. What you communicate, you teach. What you teach, you focus on. What you focus on, expands. What expands, you strengthen.

5. **ALTERNATIVES/POSSIBILITIES** You can learn to generate creative alternatives and possibilities for perceived problems in your life. Inherent within every problem is the solution. Every perceived problem has, at its root, a sense of separateness based on the "ego". Every solution has, at its root, a sense of connectedness or unity based on the higher Self. The "ego" generates a sense of separateness, difference, specialness, judgment, fear and grievances. The Self generates a sense of oneness, sameness, love and peace and frees you to

contact great strength, power, creativity and resourcefulness within you.

6. **ACCOMPLISHMENT/SATISFACTION** Accomplishment and satisfaction come from establishing a set of worthy goals in alignment with your purpose and vision in life. Fulfillment comes when you do what you love to do, when you express your talents and abilities from the creative core of your Being. Every cause has an effect. Thoughts and ideas are causes. When they arise from Self/Being as Source, they will bring you harmony, balance, peace and fulfillment. When they arise from the "ego" as source, they will bring you conflict, fear, disharmony and imbalance. What you believe, conceive and expect (causes), you will attract and achieve (effects).

7. **SELF-ESTEEM/SELF-LOVE** You are a unique person with talents, abilities, resources, and a personality that exists nowhere else. Learn to let go of negative self-talk and judgments, and to replace it with positive self-talk and affirmations. Learn to choose to be happy rather than right. Awaken from the dream; release your identification with your "ego", and learn to recognize and remember that your true Identity, your Essence/Being, is always perfect, whole and complete. It consists of love, light and beauty, is characterized by greatness and magnificence, and is the same within everyone. Yet you are a unique manifestation of this inner Light/Self.

8. **PEACE/SECURITY** Peace and security dwell within you at the core of your Being/Self. You will never find inner peace by searching outside in relationships, achievements, possessions, prestige, money, and accomplishments. The "ego" experiences itself as lacking and incomplete, so it searches for external objects or people in order to find peace. You can find peace and security by turning within to your Self/Being, by reconnecting with

your Identity/Essence. Close your eyes. Relax. Take slow, deep breaths. Then ask the creative/infinite intelligence within you to help you feel a deep sense of inner peace and security.

9. **AFFECTIONATE/LOVING RELATIONSHIPS** To create an affectionate, loving relationship, open your heart to the deep caring within you. The heart-centered response to your partner involves being kind, thoughtful and understanding of his/her needs, wants and desires. Sometimes your partner will want a hug, massage or walk in the park. Sometimes he/she will want encouragement, a receptive ear, a tender word, a good laugh, or an evening at the movies, dining or dancing. All of these communicate warmth, caring and tenderness. You can also learn to engage in more effective problem-solving with the aid of creative/infinite intelligence. What you give is what you receive. Give love and affection and you will feel it and receive it.

10. **CARING/CLOSE FRIENDSHIPS** Caring, close friendships, based on esteem, respect, appreciation and liking, develop deep bonds of affection and often love. Some of your friends will help you clarify your thinking, feelings and actions, or catalyze you to new ways of perceiving, thinking and acting. With most friends, you will uplift them when they are discouraged, or they will uplift you. Giving assistance and guidance in problem-solving, questioning and challenging you to greater growth, reminiscing with you about the past, or supporting you in pursuing dreams for the future are other major functions of friendship. With some friends, you will just play, laugh and have fun. Learn to be grateful for your friends.

11. **GRATITUDE/ABUNDANCE** More miracles occur from gratitude and forgiveness than from anything else. Love flourishes where there is gratitude and forgiveness. Be

thankful and appreciative of all the experiences, people and events in your life. To experience more gratitude, choose to be receptive to wonderful, loving and prosperous experiences, and allow yourself to experience a divine presence within you. This presence will guide you to greater experiences of love, peace, joy, sufficiency and abundance. Align yourself with this energy by releasing negative attitudes and judgments. When you do, you will experience blessings and grace entering your life.

12. **CENTER/SOURCE** A universal Source or Center dwells within you where deep love, peace, joy, fulfillment, creativity, gratitude, abundance, blessings, holiness and grace can be found. It is also the source of your inner strength, intuition, determination, compassion and resourcefulness. Sometimes the Source/Center is referred to as the inner Guide, Teacher, Master, Christ, Buddha, Jehova, Guru or Voice. The creative/infinite intelligence (divine/holy spirit or energy) can help you contact this Center. You may discover that at the core of your Source/Center is radiant light and love, and that your ultimate purpose and vision in life is to be a channel for that light and love.

KEY WORD SUMMARY OF THE TWELVE PRINCIPLES OF WELL-BEING

1. DEVELOP MEANING, PURPOSE/VISION IN LIFE

2. CREATION/MANIFESTATION OF CHOICES AND GOALS

3. POSITIVE AND FORGIVING ATTITUDES/THOUGHTS

4. POSITIVELY RE-PERCEIVE/REFRAME LIFE'S EVENTS

5. CREATIVE ALTERNATIVES/POSSIBILITIES

6. ACCOMPLISHMENT/SATISFACTION AT WORK OR HOME

7. CREATE HIGH SELF-ESTEEM/SELF-LOVE

8. DEVELOP INNER PEACE/SECURITY

9. DEVELOP AFFECTIONATE/LOVING RELATION-SHIPS

10. CREATE CARING/CLOSE FRIENDSHIPS

11. DEVELOP A SENSE OF GRATITUDE/ABUNDANCE

12. CONTACT A UNIVERSAL CENTER/SOURCE

APPENDIX I
WELL-BEING QUESTIONNAIRE

NAME_____DATE_____AGE_____

DIRECTIONS: Use the list below to answer the following ques-tion: In general, how high or low is your level of well being? Check the one statement below that best describes your average level of well-being.

____ 100. Extremely high level of well-being (Feeling ecstatic, joyous, fantastic!)

____ 90. Very high level of well-being (Feeling really good, elated!)

____ 80. Pretty high level of well-being (Spirits high, feeling good.)

____ 70. Mildly high level of well-being (Feeling fairly good and somewhat cheerful.)

____ 60. Slightly high level of well-being (Just a bit above neutral.)

____ 50. Neutral (Not particularly high or low level of well-being.)

____ 40. Slightly low level of well-being (Just a bit below neutral.)

____ 30. Mildly low level of well-being (Just a little low.)

____ 20. Pretty low level of well-being (Somewhat "blue", spirits down.)

____ 10. Very low level of well-being (Depressed, spirits very low.)

____ 00. Extremely low level of well-being (Utterly depressed, completely down.)

APPENDIX II
WELL-BEING SCALE

NAME_____DATE_____AGE_____

1.   We are interested in the way people are feeling these days. During the past few weeks, did you ever feel. . .(circle one)

   A.   Particularly excited or interested in something?   Yes   No

   B.   Proud because someone complimented you on   Yes   No
        something you had done?

   C.   Pleased about having accomplished something?   Yes   No

   D.   On top of the world?   Yes   No

   E.   That things were going your way?   Yes   No

   F.   Did you ever feel so restless that you couldn't sit still   Yes   No
        in a chair?

   G.   Very lonely or remote from other people?   Yes   No

   H.   Bored?   Yes   No

   I.   Depressed or very unhappy?   Yes   No

   J.   Upset because someone criticized you?   Yes   No

2.   The dots on the following line represent different degrees of happiness in your life. Please circle the dot which represents how happy you are these days.

●   ●   ●   ●   ●   ●   ●   ●

| Extremely Unhappy | Very Unhappy | A Little Unhappy | Neither Happy Nor Unhappy | A Little Happy | Very Happy | Extremely Happy | Perfectly Happy |

3.   Compared with your life today, how were things four or five years ago? Are things happier for you now or were they happier then? Check one.

                                          Happier now   _____
                                          About the same   _____
                                          Happier then   _____

4. Think of how your life is going now. Do you want it to continue in much the same way as it's going now; do you wish you could change some parts of it; or do you wish you could change many parts of it? Check one.

Continue much the same way _____

Change some parts_____

Change many parts_____

5. When you think of the things you want from life, would you say that you're doing pretty well or you're not doing too well now in getting the things you want? Check one.

Doing pretty well now_____

Not doing too well now_____

WELL-BEING SCALE SCORING KEY

A. 1 -   FOR A-E ITEMS: SCORE 1 FOR YES AND 0 FOR NO
          FOR F-J ITEMS: SCORE 0 FOR YES AND 1 FOR NO

B. 2 -   SCORE EXTREMELY UNHAPPY -0
          SCORE PERFECTLY HAPPY -7
          SCORE 0 TO 7 FROM LEFT TO RIGHT FOR ALL CHECK-
          MARKS IN BETWEEN EXTREMELY UNHAPPY AND PER-
          FECTLY HAPPY

C. 3-   SCORE HAPPIER NOW -1
          SCORE ABOUT THE SAME -0
          SCORE HAPPIER THEN -0

D. 4-   SCORE CONTINUE MUCH THE SAME WAY -1
          SCORE CHANGE SOME PARTS -0
          SCORE MANY PARTS -0

E. 5-   SCORE DOING PRETTY WELL -1
          SCORE NOT DOING TOO WELL -0

F. ADD SCORES FOR 3, 4 AND 5 ITEMS TOGETHER (RANGE 0-3) AND
    PUT THE SUM NEXT TO THE WORD LIFE.

G. FOR ITEM 2, PUT THE SCORE UNDER HAPP. (RANGE 0-7).

H. FOR ITEM 1, PUT THE SUM OF THE SCORES FOR ITEMS A-E
    UNDER POS. AND PUT THE SUM OF THE SCORE FOR ITEMS F-J
    UNDER NEG. (RANGE 0-5 FOR EACH).

I. ADD THE SCORE FOR POS. + NEG. TO GET SUB-TOTAL (1)
    ADD THE SCORE FOR HAPP. + LIFE TO GET SUB-TOTAL (2)
    ADD SUB-TOTAL (1) AND SUB-TOTAL (2) TO GET THE GRAND
    TOTAL. MULTIPLY THE GRAND TOTAL BY 5 TO GET THE TOTAL
    SCORE. THE SCORES WILL RANGE FROM 0 AT THE LOW END TO
    100 AT THE HIGH END.

SCORING KEY SUMMARY

                  POS._____
                  NEG._____
        SUB-TOTAL(1)_____
                 HAPP._____
                 LIFE_____
        SUB-TOTAL(2)_____
        GRAND TOTAL _____ x 5
        TOTAL SCORE_____

APPENDIX III
STRESS REACTION QUESTIONNAIRE

NAME_____DATE_____AGE_____

Below is a list of problems and complaints that people sometimes have. Read each one carefully, and select one of the numbered descriptions that best describes HOW MUCH DISCOMFORT THAT PROBLEM HAS CAUSED YOU DURING THE PAST SEVEN DAYS, INCLUDING TODAY. Place that number in the blank to the right of the problem. If you change your mind, erase your first number completely. Read the example below before beginning.

EXAMPLE:

HOW MUCH WERE YOU DISTRESSED BY:

Body Aches _____3_____

0 -- NOT AT ALL
1 -- A LITTLE BIT
2 -- MODERATELY
3 -- QUITE A BIT
4 -- EXTREMELY

1. Headaches _____
2. Faintness or dizziness _____
3. Pains in heart or chest _____
4. Pains in lower back _____
5. Nausea or upset stomach _____
6. Soreness of your muscles _____
7. Trouble getting your breath _____
8. Hot or cold spells _____
9. Numbness or tingling in parts of your body _____
10. A lump in your throat _____
11. Feeling weak in parts of your body _____
12. Heavy feelings in your arms or legs _____
13. Loss of sexual interest or pleasure _____
14. Feeling low in energy or slowed down _____
15. Thoughts of ending your life _____
16. Crying easily _____

17. Feeling of being caught or trapped _____
18. Blaming yourself for things _____
19. Feeling lonely _____
20. Feeling blue _____
21. Worrying too much about things _____
22. Feeling no interest in things _____
23. Feeling hopeless about the future _____
24. Feeling everything is an effort _____
25. Feelings of worthlessness _____
26. Nervousness or shakiness inside _____
27. Trembling _____
28. Suddenly scared for no reason _____
29. Feeling fearful _____
30. Heart pounding or racing _____
31. Feeling tense or keyed up _____
32. Spells of terror or panic _____
33. Feeling so restless you couldn't sit still _____
34. The feeling that something bad is going to happen to you _____
35. Thoughts and images of a frightening nature _____
36. Feeling easily annoyed or irritated _____
37. Temper outbursts that you could not control _____
38. Having urges to beat, injure or harm someone _____
39. Having urges to break or smash things _____
40. Getting into frequent arguments _____
41. Shouting or throwing things _____
                  TOTAL SCORE _____

APPENDIX IV
INTERPRETING THE SCORES ON THE WELL-BEING SCALE AND THE STRESS REACTION QUESTIONNAIRE

WELL-BEING SCALE

00	–	EXTREMELY LOW LEVEL OF WELL-BEING
01-15	–	VERY LOW LEVEL OF WELL-BEING
16-30	–	LOW LEVEL OF WELL-BEING
31-45	–	MODERATELY LOW LEVEL OF WELL-BEING
46-59	–	SLIGHTLY BELOW AVERAGE LEVEL OF WELL-BEING
60-69	–	AVERAGE LEVEL OF WELL-BEING
70-79	–	ABOVE AVERAGE LEVEL OF WELL-BEING
80-89	–	HIGH LEVEL OF WELL-BEING
90-99	–	VERY HIGH LEVEL OF WELL-BEING
100	–	EXTREMELY HIGH LEVEL OF WELL-BEING

STRESS REACTION QUESTIONNAIRE

0-3	–	VERY LOW LEVEL OF STRESS
4-15	–	AVERAGE LEVEL OF STRESS
16-35	–	ABOVE AVERAGE LEVEL OF STRESS
36-55	–	MODERATELY HIGH LEVEL OF STRESS
56-70	–	HIGH LEVEL OF STRESS
71-85	–	VERY HIGH LEVEL OF STRESS
> 85	–	EXTREMELY HIGH LEVEL OF STRESS

SUGGESTED READING

I would like to thank all the authors of the books listed below for their contribution to my life and for their contribution to the enhancement of the personal, relational and spiritual well-being of millions of people on the planet. Their thinking has clarified, influenced, supported, reinforced or uplifted my thinking and I want to express my appreciation to them. I would invite and encourage you to consider reading several of them on topics that appeal to you. You will surely find, as I have, that they further enrich your wisdom and well-being.

Assagioli, Roberto. *The Act of Will*
Assagioli, Roberto. *Psychosynthesis*
Bach, George. *The Inner Enemy*
Bach, George. *A Time For Caring*
Bloomfield, Harold. *Making Peace With Your Parents*
Boszormenyi-Nagy and Krasner, Barbara. *Between Give and Take*
Bradburn, Norman. *The Structure of Psychological Well-Being*
Burns, David. *Feeling Good*
Campbell, Angus. *The Sense of Well-Being in America*
Carey, Ken. *Starseed Transmissions*
Carey, Ken. *Vision*
Chidvilasananda, Gurumayi. *Kindle My Heart's Flame*. Vol. 1
Chidvilasananda, Gurumayi. *Kindle My Heart's Flame*. Vol. 2
Cohen, Alan. *The Dragon Doesn't Live Here Anymore*
Cohen, Alan. *The Healing of the Planet Earth*
Cohen, Alan. *Rising In Love*
Colt, Lee. *Listening*
Foundation For Inner Peace. *A Course In Miracles*
Frankl, Victor. *Man's Search for Meaning*
Fritz, Robert. *The Path Of Least Resistance*
Gawain, Shakti. *Creative Visualization*
Gawain, Shakti. *Living In The Light*
Guerney, Bernard. *Relationship Enhancement*
Hay, Louise. *You Can Heal Your Life*
Helmsteder, Shad. *What To Say When You Talk To Yourself*
Helmsteder, Shad. *The Self-Talk Solution*

Hill, Napolean. *Grow Rich! With Peace of Mind*
Hill, Napolean, et. al. *Success Through A Positive Mental Attitude*
Jampolsky, Gerald. *Good-bye to Guilt*
Jampolsky, Gerald. *Love is Letting Go of Fear*
Jampolsky, Gerald. *Teach Only Love*
Jampolsky, Gerald. *Out of Darkness Into The Light*
Lazaris. *Lazaris Interviews: Book 1*
Lazaris. *Lazaris Interviews: Book 2*
Lazaris. *The Sacred Journey. You And Your Higher Self*
Lazarus, Arnold. *In The Mind's Eye*
Lazarus, Arnold. *I Can If I Want To*
Lazarus, Richard and Folkman, S. *Stress, Appraisal and Coping*
Leider, Richard. *The Power of Purpose*
Levine, Stephen. *Who Dies?*
Levine, Stephen. *Healing Into Life and Death*
Maslow, Abraham. *The Farther Reaches of Human Nature*
Maslow, Abraham. *Toward a Psychology of Being*
McKay, Matthew and Fleming, Patrick. *Self-Esteem*
Miller, Sherod, et. al. *Straight Talk*
Muktananda, Swami. *I Have Become Alive*
Muktananda, Swami. *The Play of Consciousness*
Muktananda, Swami. *Siddha Meditation*
Muktananda, Swami. *Where Are You Going?*
O'Hanlon, William Hudson. *Taproots*
Olson, David, et. al. *Families. What Makes Them Work?*
Patent, Arnold. *You Can Have It All*
Peale, Norman Vincent. *Positive Imaging*
Peale, Norman Vincent. *Why Some Positive Thinkers Get Positive Results*
Pearce, Joseph Chilton. *The Bond of Power*
Ponder, Catherine. *The Dynamic Laws of Prosperity*
Porter, Grady & Lippman, Glenda. *Conversations with JC: Vol. 1*
Porter, Grady & Lippman, Glenda. *Conversations with JC: Vol. 2*
Prather, Hugh. *The Quiet Answer*
Prather, Hugh. *There Is A Place Where You Are Not Alone*
Price, John. *The Abundance Book*
Price, John. *The Manifestation Process*
Price, John. *Practical Spirituality*
Ram Dass and Gorman, Paul. *How Can I Help?*
Ray, Sandra. *Loving Relationships*
Rodegast, Pat and Stanton, Judith. *Emmanuel's Book*
Rolfe, Randy. *You Can Postpone Anything But Love*

Roman, Sanaya. *Living With Joy*
Roman, Sanaya. *Personal Power Through Awareness*
Roman, Sanaya. *Spiritual Growth*
Roman, Sanaya and Packer, Duane. *Creating Money*
Rothschild, Helene, et. al. *Free To Fly: Dare To Be A Success*
Schwartz, Stephen. *The Compassionate Presence*
Semigran, Candy. *250 Ways To Enhance Your Self-Esteem*
Shealy, Norman and Myss, Caroline. *The Creation of Health*
Sheehy, Gail. *Pathfinders*
Siegel, Bernie. *Love, Medicine and Miracles*
Simonton, Carl and Stephanie Mathews. *Getting Well Again*
The Pink Books. *Love Answers All*
The Pink Books. *The Dawning Of The Age Of Light*
Tuttle, Paul. *Conversations with RAJ*
Tuttle, Paul. *You Are The Answer*
Vissell, Barry and Vissell, Joyce. *The Shared Heart*
Waitley, Denis. *The Joy of Working*
Walsh, Roger and Vaughn, Frances. *Beyond Ego*
Wapnick, Gloria and Kenneth. *Awaken From The Dream*
Wapnick, Kenneth. *The Obstacles To Peace*
Weinberg, Stephen Lee (Ed.). *Ramtha*
Wilbur, Ken. *Spectrum of Consciousness*
Young, Meredith Lady. *Agartha*

ABOUT THE AUTHOR

Dr. Philip Friedman is a licensed psychologist with a private practice in Philadelphia and Plymouth Meeting, Pennsylvania, and the Executive Director of the Foundation for Well-Being. He received his B.A. from Columbia College in 1963 and his M.A. (1965) and Ph.D. (1968) from the University of Wisconsin. His Masters thesis was on "Social Class Differences in Social Responsibility Behavior (Altruism)". His Ph.D. thesis was on "The Effects of Modeling and Roleplaying On Assertive Behavior". He came to the Philadelphia area on a NIMH post-doctoral fellowship in 1968 to study cognitive-behavioral and multi-modal therapy at Temple University Medical School. In 1969, Phil joined the staff of the Family Psychiatry Division of Eastern Pennsylvania Psychiatric Institute and taught family systems theory and therapy in addition to conducting a clinical practice in family therapy.

In 1972, he began a spiritual search that led him to study many different spiritual disciplines and eventually to the writing of *Creating Well-Being: The Healing Path To Love, Peace, Self-Esteem and Happiness*. From 1973 to 1983, he was Director of Training in Marital and Family Therapy at Jefferson and C.A.T.C.H. Community Mental Health Centers and, for many of those years, Assistant Professor on the faculty of Jefferson Medical School. In 1977, he wrote an important article entitled "Integrative Psychotherapy". Phil entered full-time private practice in 1983 and in the same year founded, with his wife Teresa, and directed the Attitudinal Healing Center of the Delaware Valley. In 1987, following his inner guidance, he founded the Foundation for Well-Being.

In addition to writing *Creating Well-Being: The Healing Path To Love, Peace, Self-Esteem and Happiness*, Dr. Friedman has published over 30 articles in professional journals, magazines and books on a wide variety of topics, including attitude and behavior change, techniques of marital and family therapy, metaphors and models of psychotherapy, the use of computers in psychotherapy, purpose and vision in life, creating and manifesting what you want, enhancing relationships, intuition, channelled guidance, and the Twelve Principles of Well-Being. He is also an Assistant Professor at Hahnemann Medical School and University, an Approved Supervisor for the American Association of Marital and Family Therapists, the co-founder of the Integrative Interest Group, and the founder of the Spirituality Interest Group for the American Family Therapy Association's annual conference. He frequently presents workshops at local, state and national professional conferences, and for industry, universities, health care and personal/spiritual growth organizations.

Dr. Friedman has been married since 1965 to his bright, multi-talented wife, Teresa Molinaro-Friedman, a stamp dealer, and has a son Mathew, who is majoring in political communication at George Washington University. He has a private practice of psychotherapy for individuals, couples and families, and frequently conducts seminars for the public on creating and enhancing well-being, forgiveness, gratitude, love and healing. He can be contacted by writing in care of the Foundation for Well-Being, P. O. Box 627, Plymouth Meeting, Pennsylvania 19462, or by calling 215-828-4674.

ABOUT THE FOUNDATION FOR WELL-BEING

The Foundation for Well-Being was founded in Plymouth Meeting, Pennsylvania on January 1, 1987, by its Executive Director, Philip H. Friedman, Ph.D. The purpose of the Foundation is to:

1. Clarify the basic foundations or building blocks of well-being.
2. Present these building blocks to the public in the form of twelve "Core Principles of Well-Being".
3. Develop easily administered and scored measures of well-being.
4. Create a series of processes and exercises to greatly enhance the overall well-being (emotional, psychological, physical, relational and spiritual) of individuals, couples, families and groups.
5. Develop a series of seminars, workshops, courses and private consultations (utilizing an integrative, psycho-spiritual approach) to assist people in creating high levels of well-being in their lives.
6. Create a vision of organizations, institutions, corporations, and city governments that support the well-being of their members.
7. Create a vision of a society and world that aligns itself in supporting the well-being of its members.

Information about seminars, courses, workshops or private consultations can be attained by writing:

c/o Foundation for Well Being
P.O. Box 627
Plymouth Meeting, Pennsylvania 19462, or
calling 215-828-4674.

To be placed on the mailing list, write or call the above address or telephone number.

INDEX

ORDER BLANK

AUDIOTAPES	PRICE
1. MEDITATION/RELAXATION: JOURNEY TO THE INNER SANCTUARY	$11.00
2. CREATING AND MANIFESTING WHAT YOU WANT (BASIC VERSION)	$11.00
3. CREATING AND MANIFESTING WHAT YOU WANT (BRIEF VERSION AND ADVANCED VERSION-INNER JOURNEY FROM DIVINE LOVE)	$11.00
4. FORGIVENESS EXERCISE	$11.00
5. INNER JOURNEY TO THE HIGHER SELF	$11.00
6. SELF-ESTEEM	$11.00
FOR ALL SIX TAPES (REDUCED PRICE)	$63.00
SUBTOTAL	_____
Postage and handling (Add $2.00 for the first item and $.50 for each additional item.)	_____
Pennsylvania Residents add 6% sales tax	_____
TOTAL PAYMENT WITH ORDER	_____

(Make checks payable to the FOUNDATION FOR WELL-BEING)

NAME _____

ADDRESS _____

CITY, STATE, ZIP _____

VISA OR MASTERCARD NO. _____

EXPIRATION DATE _____

SIGNATURE _____

TELEPHONE: (DAY) _____ (EVENING) _____

SEND TO:
FOUNDATION FOR WELL-BEING
P. O. BOX 627
PLYMOUTH MEETING, PENNSYLVANIA 19462

VISA OR MASTERCARD CAN ONLY BE USED FOR ORDERS OF $60.00 OR MORE. FOR INFORMATION ON SEMINARS AND WORKSHOPS, PRIVATE CONSULTATIONS, OR ANY OTHER COMMUNICATION, WRITE THE ABOVE ADDRESS OR CALL 215-828-4674.

Prices are subject to change without notice.

ORDER BLANK

AUDIOTAPES	PRICE
1. MEDITATION/RELAXATION: JOURNEY TO THE INNER SANCTUARY	$11.00
2. CREATING AND MANIFESTING WHAT YOU WANT (BASIC VERSION)	$11.00
3. CREATING AND MANIFESTING WHAT YOU WANT (BRIEF VERSION AND ADVANCED VERSION- INNER JOURNEY FROM DIVINE LOVE)	$11.00
4. FORGIVENESS EXERCISE	$11.00
5. INNER JOURNEY TO THE HIGHER SELF	$11.00
6. SELF-ESTEEM	$11.00
FOR ALL SIX TAPES (REDUCED PRICE)	$63.00
SUBTOTAL	_____
Postage and handling (Add $2.00 for the first item and $.50 for each additional item.)	_____
Pennsylvania Residents add 6% sales tax	_____
TOTAL PAYMENT WITH ORDER	_____

(Make checks payable to the FOUNDATION FOR WELL-BEING)

NAME _____

ADDRESS _____

CITY, STATE, ZIP _____

VISA OR MASTERCARD NO. _____

EXPIRATION DATE _____

SIGNATURE _____

TELEPHONE: (DAY) _____ (EVENING) _____

SEND TO:
FOUNDATION FOR WELL-BEING
P. O. BOX 627
PLYMOUTH MEETING, PENNSYLVANIA 19462

VISA OR MASTERCARD CAN ONLY BE USED FOR ORDERS OF $60.00 OR MORE. FOR INFORMATION ON SEMINARS AND WORKSHOPS, PRIVATE CONSULTATIONS, OR ANY OTHER COMMUNICATION, WRITE THE ABOVE ADDRESS OR CALL 215-828-4674.

Prices are subject to change without notice.